S0-AAC-614

DISCARD

UNDERSEA EXPLORER

The Story of Captain Cousteau

UNDERSEA EXPLORER

THE STORY OF CAPTAIN COUSTEAU

BY JAMES DUGAN

*With a Message to Young People
by Captain Jacques-Yves Cousteau*

ILLUSTRATED WITH
PHOTOGRAPHS AND DIAGRAMS

HARPER & ROW, PUBLISHERS
New York   and   Evanston

UNDERSEA EXPLORER: The Story of Captain Cousteau
Copyright © 1957 by James Dugan
Printed in the United States of America

All rights in this book are reserved.
No part of this book may be used or reproduced in
any manner whatsoever without written permission
except in the case of brief quotations embodied in
critical articles and reviews. For information address
Harper & Row, Publishers, Incorporated
49 East 33rd Street, New York 16, N. Y.

The photographs appearing on
pages 77 and 84, in the color insert
between pages 80 and 81, and on the
jacket, Copyright © 1956 by Columbia
Pictures Corporation, are used with
the permission and consent of Columbia
Pictures Corporation, distributor of
the motion picture THE SILENT WORLD.

Library of Congress catalog card number: 57-9271

To
Daniel P. Cousteau

780073

750073

Contents

Illustrations

ix

Submarine Scooters haul explorers on long surveys of the bottom.

Alberto Falco hitches a ride on the back of a giant sea turtle.

Frédéric Dumas feeds scraps of food to the fish along Assumption Reef.

Jean Delmas pets the grouper which adopted the *Calypso* divers.

Ulysses, the big grouper, blunders into the undersea studio.

Ulysses keeps the divers company near the surface as they decompress.

(Black and white photographs and line drawings)

A MESSAGE TO YOUNG PEOPLE

James Dugan was the first foreigner to join Calypso Expeditions. He has voyaged with us in the Mediterranean, Red Sea, Persian Gulf, and Indian Ocean, and helped us make the film, *The Silent World*. He understands the spirit of what we are trying to do underwater. I am glad that he decided to write the story for young people, the undersea explorers of tomorrow. I hope our experience will help you avoid our errors, bypass the experiments we had to work out from scratch, and that you will have as great an enjoyment as we have had in the wonderful sea.

Diving is safe, it is fascinating, and it gives greater rewards to lively human curiosity than any other venture I know. But some people get in trouble underwater because they do not prepare for the adventure. No one should dive without knowing the basic physiology of diving and breathing under pressure. You should know how your breathing device works. And you must study the Diving Tables which tell you exactly how long you can spend at various depths.

On the *Calypso*, after thousands of dives among us, we still feel that it is a privilege to go inside the sea. Some divers do not respect the sea and go down to show off. They boast of going the deepest and staying the longest. This is a sure way to get in trouble. Physical laws govern the depth and time of dives, laws that cannot be broken.

I am often asked, "How long can you stay down with the Aqua-Lung?" It is impossible to answer the question without going into very important details on all the factors that rule the duration of a dive. You *must* have a diving manual before going down. You must read carefully about the three main dangers of diving. The first is air embolism, then nitrogen narcosis, and, lastly, the famous "bends." All three can be easily avoided when you know about them and use the Diving Tables printed in all good manuals.

A golden rule of safe diving is never to go down alone. On the *Calypso* we will not have lone rangers. We manage to dive in pairs. During the dive, the two men always keep an eye on each other, never stray from each other's sight, and are ever-ready to go to each other's aid. Mountain climbers use such a golden rule, when they rope themselves together *en cordée*. Divers should not use ropes that may become fouled, but should feel morally attached to each other. Climbing and diving free us from selfishness; they build true men. Diving is a glorious team sport, best enjoyed when discoveries are shared among the group. The finest divers travel in schools, like fish.

Philippe Tailliez, Frédéric Dumas, and I started down together twenty years ago. I am sure that the knowledge we shared developed each one of us faster than solo diving would have done. Dumas brought his underwater swimming techniques, his scouting talent. Tailliez gave us his imaginative and creative view of the sea. As the diving team expanded from three to a hundred, it was always teamwork that led us on.

Today, there are scores of thousands of divers around the

world and more thousands discovering the grand adventure every day. This is the golden age of underwater exploration. Those who find the most fun and do the best work are the people who learn the laws beforehand and develop their techniques as a team.

JACQUES-YVES COUSTEAU

First of the Menfish

A LONE SWIMMER cruised the green-blue sea off Tunisia. About all you could see of him was the slow flutter of his rubber foot fins and his breathing tube sticking out of the water. He was looking down through his diving mask at unknown landscapes on the sea floor. He was Lieutenant Jacques-Yves Cousteau of the French Navy, one of the first of the menfish. The time was the summer of 1939. On leave from his cruiser, Cousteau had come to explore the mysterious African seas. He had almost lived underwater since he had started to dive three years before with his friends, Philippe Tailliez and Frédéric Dumas.

Looking through the clear depths, Cousteau saw, thirty feet below, a strange, flat stony floor with deep holes in it. He pelted down and stuck his head in a hole. He saw an astonishing scene. The floor was completely hollow underneath. It was a sort of platform standing on natural pillars. The true sand bottom was three feet deeper. In the gloom beneath the false bottom, thousands of fish weaved slow

Claude Houlbrecque

1. During the early mask-diving days Dumas and Cousteau warmed themselves by beach fires to restore lost caloric heat.

dances around the pillars. Fifty feet away Cousteau saw a shaft of sunlight coming through another hole. The fish shone gold and silver as they passed through the distant light.

He returned to the surface with a head full of ideas. On the next dive he passed through his hole and let fly at a fish. He came up with two fish on his spear. He was fascinated with the secret place beneath the floor and wondered how he could explore it. He had no breathing apparatus to stay down. But perhaps a diver could swim in one hole and out the other, while holding his breath.

He rested in the sun, planning the lonely plunge. It was his habit to think out every move of a difficult dive before he went down. He figured it would not take long to get through the first hole, forty seconds to swim beneath the floor to the other hole, and a few seconds to get back to the surface. This would be at a slow pace, giving him time to look around under the false bottom, and still have a good margin of safety. In a pinch he could hold his breath for two minutes underwater.

The decision was made. He took a big lungful of air and plunged, swimming down slowly to save his breath. As he knifed through the golden-green water, his chest shrank in increasing water pressure. He disappeared through the first hole, from brightness to twilight. He leveled off, facing the escape hole, and surveyed the intervening space for obstacles. Had there been any, his plan called for returning through the entrance hole. The coast was clear.

Cousteau struck out for the beam of light, against which schools of fish were silhouetted like leaves. They parted before him and he felt their fins brush his back. He picked up a sample of rock and arrived at the exit hole in forty seconds, according to schedule. He stuck his head up through the hole, put his fins on the floor in a crouch, and sprang for the surface. His shoulders jarred against the hole. It was entirely too narrow to get through.

His blithe self-confidence vanished. Cousteau was trapped under the floor with a half minute to live. It was too far back to the entrance hole. His lungs were accumulating deadly carbon dioxide, the product of his own breath. With his head through the hole, and his heart beating hard, he tried to face the problem coolly. His hundreds of dives had taught him that losing your head was the finish. Faintly he remembered that, as he had arrived at the trap, there had been another hole nearby, another sunny spot. It was his only chance for life.

If the next hole was not large enough, he would soon die, a victim of curiosity and daring. He ducked under the floor and popped through the third hole, lacerating his naked body in the jump for life.

Cousteau said, "That dive taught me a lot. Never again would I try a foolish stunt like that. I wanted to know what was under the false bottom and was trying to prove I could do it in one breath. But my planning was no good. I didn't check the escape hole beforehand. The main lesson was that free divers had to have breathing apparatus so they would not be trapped by time. Dumas, Tailliez and I saw tantalizing things down there, but we never could stay long enough to study them. We needed breathing apparatus. It was a pretty sore point with me, because I had already built two oxygen lungs that nearly killed me."

In 1938, while serving as a gunner on the cruiser *Pluton*, Cousteau designed an oxygen rebreathing lung, which was built by his gunsmith out of a brass box and a motorcycle inner tube, which fitted around the diver's waist and served as the breathing bag. Cousteau used the standard principle of the oxygen lungs already used for escaping from sunken submarines. The diver's exhalations passed back into the bag and were repurified in soda lime to be breathed again.

Cousteau tested the oxygen lung from a boat manned by two sailors. At last he felt the long-hoped-for thrill of swimming underwater for many minutes. The silent apparatus was a magic carpet for flying the skies beneath the world. He invaded a submerged cavern and backed a fish into a corner. It wriggled past him and escaped. He left the cave and started after a big bream forty-five feet down. The experts had told him oxygen was safe to that depth, but below forty-five feet you were liable to have oxygen convulsions and lose consciousness. By now he had been down a full half hour, breathing pure oxygen, overjoyed with the liberty of the sea. Suddenly his lips started to tremble around the mouthpiece. His eyelids blinked wildly. His spine bent backward. He knew it was a violent oxygen convulsion and that he would pass out in an instant. As he recognized the symptoms, his hands ripped off his ten-pound belt weight. He floated unconscious to the surface and was fished out alive.

Cousteau did not know that the experts were wrong and oxygen could be deadly when breathed at only thirty-three feet down. He thought the accident was due to poor design of his apparatus. He built a new oxygen lung and tested it early in 1939. He convulsed so quickly that he does not even remember slipping his belt weights. After that he was through with the serene and treacherous gas.

The False-Bottom Dive demanded a new attempt at breathing gear, with compressed air, perhaps. Helmet divers were being lowered to two hundred feet, breathing compressed air through their air pipes to the surface. . . . Cousteau was studying the method when World War II came and cut off the project.

Twelve hours a day Cousteau was in charge of the central artillery calculator on the cruiser *Dupleix,* one of the French and British "X" Force hunting the German pocket battleship *Graf Spee* in the Atlantic. During hasty turn-arounds in port, he got in some naked dives. One day the *Dupleix* had to stop for engine repairs in the Sargasso Sea. Cousteau had often imagined what it would be like to dive under the floating weed gardens of the Sargasso. And here it was. The legends said sunken pirate cutters and Spanish galleons were floating under this snarl of weed. He did not believe that; the place held facts stranger than pirate tales: the life history of the European eel.

A Danish scientist, Johannes Schmidt, spent his life solving the fantastic riddle of the eel, which lives in both fresh and salt water. As old ocean eels are about to die they swim to the Sargasso Sea. Two miles below the floating weeds, the eels mate and die. The young are born as transparent larva, which drift far away in the deep currents of the Atlantic, and grow into little eels, or elvers. The elvers swim up the river and into lakes in Europe and North America. When they are grown, they become silver eels and return to the ocean. Finally all eels swim back to the Sargasso Sea and breed and die.

The masked, naked man went down the high gray side of the cruiser and disappeared in the weeds, like a man diving into a vacant lot. Cousteau flipped down and found that the mat of vegetation was only a foot thick. Myriads of tiny sea animals dwelt on the roots of the plants. As he skinned beneath the garden, his ears reverberated with the clash and clank of the engine-room artificers in the steel city of the *Dupleix*. Cousteau looked down toward the birthing room and cemetery of eels. The water was crystal clear fathom upon fathom down, but the country of the eels was beyond human sight.

He climbed back aboard and the *Dupleix* sped for Dakar. There he took a shipmate named Chopard on his first undersea hunt with slingshot harpoons. They dived from a native boat into poor visibility. Cousteau sensed the approach of a lordly animal. It was a ten-foot tiger shark that passed him by a foot. He popped up and looked for Chopard. The novice appeared, yelling for help, and sank immediately. Cousteau went down and hauled him up, prepared for a gory sight as he boosted Chopard into the boat. Instead, he burst out laughing. The shark had not struck Chopard. His legs were trapped in the big rubber bands of his harpoon gun.

One day the outcome wasn't so funny. Cousteau was teaching a green diver, who missed his fish and ran his spear into Cousteau's leg.

When Paris fell to the Germans in 1940, the French Mediterranean fleet became less active. Cousteau had time

to return to the problem of compressed air, the only thing
to breathe if he was to attain his dream of menfish roving
beneath the waves. He was working on the theory when the
Germans rolled into southern France in November, 1942.
The French sank their fleet to keep it from the enemy and
Cousteau was discharged with his fellow sailors. In this
time of lowest hope and despair for his country, Cousteau
started to work full time on the air lung. Within two months,
he had the first Aqua-Lung, the invention that opened the
golden age of undersea exploration.

CHAPTER II

Window in the Ocean

THE INGENUITY THAT led to the Aqua-Lung showed early in Cousteau's life. When he was eleven, he borrowed the blueprints of a two-hundred-ton floating crane and built a four-foot electric-powered model with his Meccano set. His father showed the model to a marine engineer, who said, "Monsieur Cousteau, did you help your son build it?" The father said, "No, he did it all by himself." "Well," said the engineer, "the boy has added a useful movement that is not in the big crane. If he keeps it up, he might be a real inventor."

Jacques-Yves Cousteau was born in 1910 at his family's country place at Saint-André-de-Cubzac, near the port of Bordeaux. His father was an international businessman, always on the move.

Jacques-Yves Cousteau went from one school to another, following his father's movements. In the summers the Cousteau family lived in a seashore villa at Royan on the Atlantic. There the boy took to the water and became a fine swimmer.

2. The future undersea explorer at the age of eleven years.

When he was ten the family lived in New York for a year in an apartment house at Broadway and Ninety-sixth Street. Young Cousteau ran the streets with the West Side kids, who called him Jack. He played stickball, potsy and other traditional Manhattan games; captured the snow forts, and went to a summer camp in Vermont run by two Yale professors. A camp counselor noticed he was a good swimmer and asked him if he thought he could clear out the dead branches on the bottom of the lake under the diving board. It was a good dare: the water was twelve feet deep. The boy grinned and ducked under. There were no diving masks in those days. Everything he saw was a blur. Jack kept at it and removed all the dead wood. However, he was not very much interested in surface diving, simply because he couldn't see clearly underwater.

When he was thirteen he wrote a book called *An Adventure in Mexico*. He lettered and illustrated the book by hand, ran it through a mimeograph machine and bound it. His father noticed that Jack's studies were being neglected. In the boy's room he found a stack of printed stationery: "FILMS ZIX, Jack Cousteau, producer, director and chief cameraman."

When Jacques-Yves came home, M. Cousteau said, "Where did you get the movie camera?" He said, "I saved up for it." M. Cousteau said, "Well, you'd better let me keep it, until you catch up in school." The boy won the camera back the next month. Later he admitted, "My films weren't much good. What I liked was taking the camera apart and developing my own film."

Jacques-Yves already spoke English. He perfected his

German at a school at Ribeauville in Alsace. From the age
of fifteen his parents allowed him to go alone on summer
holidays in England, Germany and Spain to learn other
people's languages and ways.

When he left school Cousteau entered Stanislas College
in Paris to prepare for the Naval Academy. He plunged deep
into the books, but was taunted by the feats of his older
brother, Pierre, as a rugby player and decided to go out for
the Stanislas rugby team. He made the "pack," which is
something like the line in American football. Rugby is a
body-crashing game like football, but the players wear no
helmets or padding, play in shorts and there are fifteen men
on each side, playing the whole game without substitutions.

The skinny Cousteau brother took a terrible walloping.
He said, "I did my best. I was very careful to stay away from
the ball. If you ever got the ball, twenty-nine people
crashed into you." At the end of the season brother Pierre
opened the sports paper, *l'Equipe,* to see if he had made the
All-Paris School Rugby Team. His eyes popped when he
saw a team picture captioned, "Stanislas College XV,
Schoolboy Champions of Paris." Jacques-Yves was standing
a good distance from the ball, grinning maliciously, thought
Pierre. But Pierre had made the All-Paris Team, which
eased the shock.

Jacques-Yves entered the Naval Academy at Brest as
No. 22 of a thousand candidates. His class had glorious
luck: they were sent on a one-year cruise around the world
on the schoolship, *Jeanne d'Arc,* the first time that had happened to French cadets. Cousteau explored the wilds of
Borneo, San Francisco and New York. In the fabulous port

3. While an aviation cadet, Cousteau loved to ski in the Alps.

of Muscat in Oman, Arabia, he and his pals scaled the harbor cliffs and painted "Jeanne d'Arc" in huge letters. (Twenty-two years later, he sailed into Muscat on his own ship, the *Calypso,* and "Jeanne d'Arc" was still plainly visible among the hundreds of warship names.)

Cousteau was graduated No. 2 in his Naval Academy class and became chief officer of the French Naval Base at Shanghai. When he got back to France his restless drive for adventure interrupted a promising career as a deck officer. He entered the fleet aviation academy at Hourtin. He was about to graduate when he had an accident which was to change his life.

Alone in an open Salmson sports car Cousteau sped along a deserted mountain road at night. Fog filled the valley below and came up to the road. He seemed to be racing on a white sea. Suddenly the car plunged into a fog bank. He saw a tree coming and swerved. The car hurtled off the road and rolled over several times.

Cousteau awakened with his head jammed into the ground. He knew that several ribs were broken. The bones of his right forearm stuck out through the skin. His left arm would not move. He crawled up to the middle of the road to stop a car.

Long minutes passed and no car came. He realized that he would bleed to death if he did not get help soon. He started down the road, torturing himself with every move, fighting to stay alive. He came to a crossroads sign. It said the nearest village was four miles away. He fell back in despair. Then, through the pain, blood and fog, he heard a dog barking. He dragged himself toward the sound and came to a dark house. His cries for help were answered by an angry woman's voice. "Go away!"

Cousteau said, "Madame, if you saw me, you would not say that." She opened the door, took him in and sent her boy on a bicycle for a doctor. That night in a hospital the bones of his right forearm were shortened and set. A few days later the dead left arm became infected. The doctors said they would probably have to cut it off. Cousteau said, "I forbid you to cut it off." The broken arm was very slow to heal, but Cousteau paid all his attention to the other. He tried to move his fingers and they would not stir. Day after day, week after week, his will power ordered the fingers to move. Doctors tested the arm in the laboratory and said the radial nerve was dead. One said sympathetically, "Lieutenant, I think you should get used to the idea that you will have to wear a brace." The patient said, "I can't accept that." He put the arm in whirlpool baths and fought the dead fingers like an enemy he wanted to capture alive. After eight months he moved one finger!

He kept at it and soon had them all moving. Today, the fingers that were not supposed to stir again serve Cousteau on delicate work like camera repairs. After his own victory over disability, Cousteau helps other handicapped people who are trying to help themselves. Today, one of his best divers on the research ship *Calypso* is a young man with a leg shriveled by polio. Another diver lost three and a half fingers in the explosion of a mine detonator. He could not get working permits on account of the crippled hand. Cousteau took him to a naval doctor. The diver hid his bad hand and passed the physical. As the doctor was signing the work-

ing papers, he spied the crippled hand. He said, "Sorry,
Captain, I can't pass this man." Cousteau said, "He is perfectly capable of carrying out every job as a seaman and
diver on the *Calypso*." The doctor finally signed a special
permit that he could work only on Cousteau's ship.

Cousteau's auto crash injuries washed him out of aviation.
It was a fateful accident: most of the other cadets in his
flying class were killed in World War II. The recuperating
officer was sent to the cruiser *Suffren* in Toulon as an in-
structor in 1936. There he met a thin, intelligent lieutenant
named Philippe Tailliez, who loved swimming as much as
Cousteau did. He noticed that swimming helped his arms
to recover. He and Tailliez swam every day in the Mediterranean and developed the fastest crawl strokes around
Toulon.

Tailliez discovered watertight swimming goggles when
they first appeared on the market. He told Cousteau, "These
things are magical. Goggles let you see everything clearly
underwater. It's a new world." Cousteau put them on and
waded out from the beach. He stuck his face under. He was
amazed to see, sharp and clear, rocks, weeds and fish that
had been vague shadows to his naked eyes. He said to a
lady who was wading with her children, "Why, there are
fish all around us!" She shuddered. "Fish?" said she. "Come,
mes enfants, let us get out of here quick!"

Cousteau looked under again and "civilization vanished
with one last bow," as he said in *The Silent World*. He knew
at that moment that the wilderness below was going to be
his life. Like Endymion in Keats's poem, "The visions of

the earth were gone and fled; He saw the giant sea above
his head."

Peering down through the goggle windows, Cousteau and
Tailliez kicked up their heels and dived. Further and further, they struggled down. Then they discovered rubber
fins, which added 40 per cent more foot power. Tailliez
made breathing tubes from garden hose so they could swim
on the surface with their faces submerged continuously,
staring inside the sea. Then they met Frédéric Dumas, a
slim diver who was further along than they in the reverse
evolution of man into fish. Dumas completed the famous
pioneer trio of free divers.

Dumas had been a sickly child, too weak to go to school.
His parents moved to Sanary-on-the-Sea, and the boy gained
his health in the water. Dumas never did go to school. Both
his parents were teachers and he passed his exams at home.

Cousteau, Tailliez and Dumas made their first underwater movie, *Sixty Feet Down,* without breathing apparatus. They had found an underwater tunnel running clear
through Magnon Reef. It was crowded with groupers—
perchlike fishes. Cousteau wanted to film Dumas spearing
a fish in the tunnel. Both would have to be in position at
exactly the same moment in the brief time they could hold
their breaths. They would have to dive from opposite sides
of the island. But there was a hill between so that they could
not see each other. They planned it successfully, never-
theless.

They took places on the shores above the tunnel mouths.
A friend stood on the peak between and signaled Cousteau
to dive. Four seconds later he signaled Dumas. In the mean-

time Cousteau was driving down to fifty feet. He trained his
camera into the cave and started it, just as Dumas came into
view on the other end. Dumas swam toward the camera
and speared the grouper on the way. Timing like this produced a film eighteen minutes long.

Again, Cousteau thought how much easier it would be
with breathing equipment!

CHAPTER III

The Aqua-Lung Adventure

IN HIS QUEST for a compressed air lung, Cousteau studied helmet diving, in which the air is pumped down a rubber pipe. Helmet divers were operating down to two hundred feet, but Cousteau disliked their clumsy suits. The heavy helmet, belt and breast weights and twenty-pound boots kept a man captive. And the lines to the surface would not let him roam.

Divers had to be free. Divers had to be fish. Why couldn't they carry compressed air tanks on their backs? Cousteau learned of a semi-independent compressed air outfit invented in 1862, but it was too limited and clumsy. Still, it was a promise. There had been other attempts at a portable diving lung since then, but none of them were fully automatic. He wanted an outfit that would feed air automatically at the right pressure for any depth the diver was in. The diver would not have to bother with the apparatus, read any gauges or turn any handles. Cousteau made calculations on an automatic air regulator, which would accomplish this

19

feat. It would be a very complicated job to make the device simple. And he was not an engineer.

He heard that there was an expert at handling gases under pressure named Émile Gagnan, who worked in Paris. In December, 1942, a month after he was discharged from the Navy during the German take-over in the South of France, Cousteau went to Paris. He found Gagnan in a laboratory at the Air Liquide Company. The pressure engineer was a dark-haired man with a shy smile. Oddly enough, his first invention, at the age of eleven, had been a model submarine that dived and came up automatically. Young Gagnan had weighted the conning tower with lumps of sugar until the boat sank. Gradually the sugar melted away and the submarine surfaced.

Cousteau told Gagnan what he wanted. The engineer smiled and handed him a rectangular device about the size of a book. "This is a regulator I made to run cars on cooking gas instead of gasoline," said Gagnan. "Your problem seems to be very similar." In those wartime days Frenchmen drove around with big cooking-gas tanks on top of their cars, using Gagnan's device.

Cousteau examined the regulator. "It's built along the lines we need," he said. "The diving regulator must give a man compressed air on his slightest intake of breath." They went to work redesigning it. In a few weeks, Cousteau and Gagnan had turned the automobile gadget into the first Aqua-Lung, the passport to inner space.

The Aqua-Lung regulator has two chambers, one wet, one dry. They are separated by a flexible wall, or diaphragm. The air intake hose from the diver's mouth enters the dry

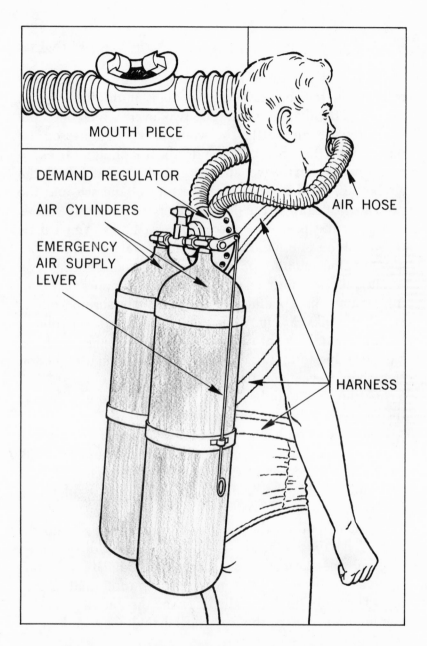

MOUTH PIECE

DEMAND REGULATOR

AIR CYLINDERS

EMERGENCY
AIR SUPPLY
LEVER

AIR HOSE

HARNESS

4. The Aqua-Lung, the Cousteau-Gagnan automatic independent
compressed-air diving apparatus, "the passport to inner space."

chamber. As you draw in a breath, it causes a slight depression in the air chamber, which is multiplied by the surface of the diaphragm and by two levers which open the high-pressure air bottles on your back. Compressed air rushes into the chamber, bends the diaphragm back to position between the wet and dry chambers, and cuts off the air bottles. At this point, the pressure of the sea and the pressure of the air in the dry chamber are exactly the same, and so is the pressure in your human lungs. You exhale through the same mouthpiece, but the stale air passes out another pipe and into the water through a non-return valve.

The process continues: diver inhaling, diaphragm bending in, air tanks opening, air and water pressure becoming equal, air tanks closing. Since 1943, there have been millions of Aqua-Lung dives around the world. Not a single accident has been due to failure of the Cousteau-Gagnan regulator. If it should ever jam, the Aqua-Lung fails safely. In such a case, the air cannot be cut off, but flows steadily, allowing the diver to make the surface.

Cousteau made history's first Aqua-Lung dive in the icy waters of the Marne River outside of Paris in January, 1943. In the first model, the exhaust valve was placed in the mouthpiece, about ten inches higher than the regulator on his back.

Gagnan stood on the bank as Cousteau waded into the river. The diver's head disappeared in the dirty water. Gagnan was alarmed to see Cousteau's exhalation coming up in a steady stream, not in the rhythm of normal breathing. Their design had failed. Then, the bubbles started coming up in bursts, the way they should. Gagnan happily watched the bubbles walk across the water. It meant Cousteau was swimming freely, breathing automatically. The design was right, after all.

The next moment Gagnan saw the bubbles cease entirely. After anxious seconds, the engineer threw off his overcoat and started untying his shoes to go after Cousteau. Before he could jump in, Cousteau appeared. Gagnan said, "*Mon Dieu,* Jacques, I thought you were drowned." Cousteau said, "I was only standing on my head." He climbed out, shivering and frowning. "The darn thing runs wide open when you are standing and it gets hard to breathe when you are upside down." Gagnan said, "Well, what happened in between? The bubbles looked okay." Cousteau said, "That's when I was swimming horizontally. Then, it works fine. But how are we going to go up and down with it?"

They drove back to Paris in silence, except for the mocking hiss of the regulator on Gagnan's gas tank. Both were thinking hard on the cause of failure. They hit it simultaneously and began shouting to each other. The reason it flowed continuously when Cousteau stood was that the exhaust was ten inches higher than the intake. Ten inches made a tremendous difference in water pressure. When Cousteau was upside down, the exhaust was ten inches lower, thus making inhalation hard. On the level swim, the two pipes were at the same pressure and the circuit worked perfectly. The solution was to place the exhaust as near the center of the diaphragm as possible. They rebuilt the regulator and rushed to an indoor tank. Cousteau dived and threw himself into crazy underwater acrobatics. The air came sweetly in every position.

Cousteau, Tailliez and Dumas eagerly awaited summer when they could take the air lung into the real sea. They could hardly wait to plunge and swim for an hour sixty feet down. At last Gagnan sent them the second well-built model and they hurried to an isolated rocky cove in the Mediterranean.

Dumas and Madame Simone Cousteau acted as safety men, looking down from the surface, as Cousteau made the first sea dive. He glided down like a man in a dream of space flight. Perfectly suspended in space, without weight, neither pulled up by buoyancy nor down by gravity, Cousteau felt the exultation of the manfish. He somersaulted and stunted like an airplane. He loafed on his back as in a gigantic featherbed. He looked up at his guards, like a fish watching seabirds. Glorious minutes passed with no need to rush to the surface to gulp air. The regulator sighed and rippled, instantly responding to his breathing, and he watched his expanding silvery bubbles soaring toward the sun.

Nearby was an undersea grotto, one of those the naked divers had so often wished they could explore. *What's to stop us now?* thought Cousteau. He swam into the cave. His exhalations pooled upside down on the ceiling, forming shining puddles of air. A puddle overflowed and a rivulet of air snaked off to find another crevice. Then he saw that there was more than puddles on the ceiling. It was crowded with small lobsters, waving their antennas. He plucked two, went up and handed them to his wife. He went up and down, handing her lobsters, enough for a triumphant feast for the diving team that night. It was a dinner of wild dreams and plans for the Aqua-Lung, but imagination could not match what was actually going to happen. They could not foresee that the automatic lung was going to open a new age of ocean science and the most exciting of sports, when millions of people went inside the sea.

Dumas thought of the invention as a way to get at sunken ships and undersea treasure. As soon as they had two lungs, they went for a sunken ship. She was a French Navy tug that had been sunk deliberately the year before to keep her from the Germans. She was only forty-five feet down, a safe depth for the device designed for sixty feet. They swam into the tug's radio room, which looked so clean and natural that the radio man might have walked in at any moment. They penetrated another suicide vessel, the torpedo boat, *Le Mars,* and were very careful because she was all of sixty-five feet down.

An officer of the *Mars* had asked Cousteau to fetch some things from his cabin. The divers swam through a ring-around-a-rosy of sea bass, penetrated fearfully into the wreck and found the officer's cabin. They opened the door easily and looked in. Cousteau said later, "His shoes were still lined up on the floor. His pencils, wooden clothes hangers, rulers and hairbrushes were up against the ceiling. It was so real, it was horrible. I couldn't stand seeing one of our ships in this state of living death. I went up without taking anything from the wreck."

Dumas, on the other hand, always grabbed souvenirs from wrecks. One was the *Dalton,* a freighter that had crashed into rocky Planier Island, near Marseille, and was lying on a slope under the rock. He found the ship's oaken wheel and started to saw it off. When he pushed the saw, instead of cutting, the stroke shoved him away. He was a weightless man, suspended in water, without body leverage. Dumas managed to loosen his souvenir after hours of work, clinging to the wheel with one hand and sawing with the other. He swam up, holding it proudly in front of him. Cousteau said, "He looked like a ghost pilot steering an invisible ship."

This *Dalton* was a challenging, frightening, magical wreck. They were venturing to seventy feet to explore her upper part. And they could see below them through the clear water, her long carcass sloping down, beckoning them, demanding to be explored. Yard by yard, apprehensive for

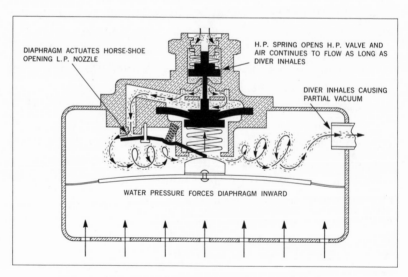

5. The Aqua-Lung regulator, from a United States Navy Diving Manual.

the untried lung, they went deeper in the *Dalton.* The Aqua-Lung went on working in each new depth.

They reminded each other they were going to depths considered dangerous for helmet divers and there was not a trained diver among them. But still they dived: ninety feet down in the dark hold of the *Dalton,* then along the main deck to the stern rail a hundred feet down. And they looked over the stern and saw the great propellers thirty feet further down. They had to go. Cousteau leaned over the rail and felt the water with his hand, as though it were empty air, through which he was about to fall into the screws. He jumped off and Dumas went with him to the propeller cage, 130 feet down. The lungs kept time to their excited breathing. What was the limit of this device? It seemed to want to go deeper and deeper. But they remained afraid that the lung was going to reach a limit, like the oxygen rig.

Tailliez discovered a big coral cave ninety feet down. He urged his friends to visit "Ali Baba's Cave," as he named it. By now they were discovering and naming places of their own in the undersea world. The earth's secret places have been found, but the sea floor is a boundless wilderness waiting for men to name its wonders.

The team dived to Ali Baba's Cave on a raw spring day, following a storm. The three underwater zealots dived in any kind of weather in their craze for discovery. But this water was almost too cold. Tailliez led his shivering friends into his cave. Inside the water was warm as toast! They tried to figure out why—each oddity they encountered led them to inquire of natural science for an explanation. The warmth of Ali Baba's Cave, they found, was due to the fact that the

warm top layer of the sea had been pushed away in the
storm and cold bottom water had welled up to take its
place. But the wind could not scoop out the cozy heat of
the cave.

Cousteau was living a doubly dangerous life at this time.
He was both underwater and underground. He was an
officer in a secret patriot group working against the occupy-
ing enemy. One time he stole the Italians' secret code book
without their finding it out.

The code was in a locked safe in Italian headquarters at
Sète. After several months of preparation Cousteau dressed
himself and three men as Italians and drove to the headquarters in a car with Italian plates. They timed their
arrival just after the Italian chief left for the day, hoping the
sentry would think Cousteau was the boss coming back for
something he had forgotten. Sure enough, the sentry saluted
as Cousteau bounded up the stairs with his men. One of
them was a locksmith. He opened the safe and Cousteau set
up a miniature camera and began copying the code book
and other top-secret papers. It took him four hours to
finish the job, but he would not quit until he had everything. Every noise might have meant alarm and capture, but
they had good nerves. At last he put the papers back, locked
them up and strolled out. The sentry saluted and they
roared away. Cousteau calls it "The dive into Italian headquarters."

CHAPTER IV

J Meet Cousteau

DURING THE WAR Dumas speared *mérous,* the Mediterranean groupers, for his hungry relatives and friends. They are rock fish weighing up to a hundred pounds. He hated to shoot them. They are intelligent animals, much interested in divers, and easy to kill. "Often, when I had stalked a *mérou* into his cave," said Dumas, "I paused before thrusting the spear, the way savages do before they slay the totem animal of their tribe."

Since those days, Cousteau's group rarely hunts fish. He says, "The diver has too big an advantage. The only honest reason for spearing them is to fill hungry bellies. Underwater, the sport is diving itself, not senseless fish-sticking."

Dumas had odd adventures with *mérous* when he was hunting for the pot. Once, on a deserted floor, he chased a little *mérou* into a rock pile. He looked in and saw the fish outlined against the waving tail of a giant *mérou.* He circled the cairn and hurled his harpoon into the big one's head. The shaft waggled violently in Dumas' grip. He braced his

feet on the rocks and hauled in the spear. The big fish fought
back. It was too big to come through the window. Dumas
tugged harder. The rock house fell down and Dumas somersaulted backward with the fifty-pounder whipping on the
spear. The little *mérou* escaped from the crash and ran like
a thief.

Another time Dumas speared and fought a big *mérou*
inside a cave eighty feet down. The fish tired him out. He
released the spear and swam out of the cave to get his
breath. Outside there was a crowd of nosy *mérous* who had
been watching the fight. He bowed and went back in for
the second round. The fish thrashed its tail and spurted sand
in his face. Instinctively he closed his eyes, although the
sand was harmlessly hitting his mask. Dumas brought the
fighter up and said, "This is some guy. He threw sand in my
face." Cousteau said, "Don't tell me your fish stories. Let's
eat." That night Dumas took a shower. He yelled for Cousteau, and combed sand and gravel out of his hair. "Fish
story, eh, Jacques?" said the hunter.

They learned that a *mérou* speared through the brain
dies instantly, but then two different things can happen.
The fish may turn white, empty its air chambers in a stream
of bubbles and sink. Or the air chambers swell and the
mérou soars to the surface. In one *mérou* he speared Dumas
found two fishhooks. One was shiny new and the other was
thickly coated. The fish had chewed off two fishing lines
many years apart.

Another time Cousteau and Dumas were ambling along
a rocky bottom ninety feet down. They came to a deep
fissure crowded with young *mérous*. They stopped and hung

over the little canyon. The fish did not seem to worry about them. Cousteau said, "They swam up toward us, turned over and glided back down, like children on a sliding board. Deeper in the crack a dozen adults strolled back and forth. One of them turned dead white, and the others passed it closely. One of the marchers stopped by the white fish and turned white as well. The two white fish rubbed against each other, while the youngsters dreamily went up and down the sliding board." Cousteau cannot explain what was happening. "There are thousands of things for divers to learn in the sea," he says, "when they get over the primitive killing idea and begin to watch, study and take pictures."

When their friends ashore asked the mysterious three what they were doing, the divers raved about the marvels they saw below. But no outsider could imagine what it was like. Films were the only way to show the travels of menfish, the flight of stingrays, octopuses traveling by jet and the dreamy rhythms of the sea.

They built an underwater 35 mm. movie camera. But they could get no film. Movie film was rationed to professional movie-makers. Cousteau got an idea. He went around to camera shops buying up miniature camera films five feet long. Madame Cousteau opened the film rolls under her bedcovers and spliced them together into hundred-foot movie lengths. She pasted together hundreds of rolls for the first Aqua-Lung movie, *Épaves,* or "Sunken Ships."

I saw this wonderful four-reel film after the liberation of Paris in 1944, and started looking for the men who made it. I was told two of them were French Navy officers, probably

stationed in the South of France. I couldn't get army orders
to go off looking for a couple of human fish. Months passed.
I was ordered to duty on *Yank* magazine in London. One
day a friend of mine named Olwen Vaughan said, "I just
saw a preview of an amazing French picture made underwater." I said, *"Épaves!"* "That's right," she said. "The producer just brought it over from France." I yelled, "Where
is he?" "At Claridge's Hotel," she answered. I took off.

Cousteau was a tall, very thin young man in the blue
uniform of a Lieutenant de Vaisseau of the French Navy.
He had a great hook of a nose and large-lidded eyes. The
face was solemn, extraordinary, a bit sad, the visage of a
poet. Then he smiled. The huge grin transformed the face
like a stick thrown in a still pond—ripples and crinkles of
fun spread over the high forehead, radiated from the eyes,
wrinkled the cheeks, and his eyeballs turned halfway up
into his head. His two faces were as different as the masks
of tragedy and comedy above a theater stage. Both were
Cousteau: the thinker and the man who gets the most fun
out of life of anyone I know.

He was glad to explain the Lung to me and report the
adventures of the diving team. He talked of what "we" did
and not about what "I" did. Dumas, Tailliez and Gagnan,
his navy comrades, his friend Roger Gary, stood out in the
tale. Working with Cousteau in the years since, I think his
feeling for teamwork is what sets him apart from other explorers. Some are as dauntless and skillful as Cousteau, but
none have built on comradeship alone an organization that
could match the one he has today.

I listened to him for hours in that first meeting. Here was

6. The original manfish trio and friends in 1940. Second from left in back row is Philippe Tailliez, then Roger Gary, Cousteau and friend. Front row, left to right: Claude Houlbrecque (now a United Nations film-maker) and Frédéric Dumas.

an epic never printed, and I was the first reporter to get it. I checked my article with a U. S. Navy diving officer. He said, "This Aqua-Lung is possible, but not probable." I said, "But I have seen a long movie of Cousteau's outfit swimming around like fish. You can tell they are down deep. You don't see any dancing light from the waves." The officer said, "I wouldn't care to try it." He did not contradict any of the technical points. But no magazine would print the story for three years.

In 1948, Jack Horner, my former editor on *Yank*, started a new magazine called *Science Illustrated*. He printed the Cousteau story. Hundreds of people wrote in, asking where they could get Aqua-Lungs. One of the letters was from Commander Francis Douglas Fane, leader of U. S. Navy underwater demolition teams, which were using oxygen lungs. Fane got some Aqua-Lungs and the frogmen loved them. Today, thirteen navies use the Aqua-Lung.

You will never see the first Aqua-Lung in a museum. During the war, Cousteau kept it in a Marseille paint factory owned by Roger Gary. When the Allies landed in Marseille in 1944, some Germans tried to hold out in a fort miles from the factory. The Allies sent a warning, "Come out or we'll blast you out." The Germans refused. The guns opened up. Somebody was not pointing his gun very straight. A shell hit Gary's factory and blew up the first Lung.

In our first meeting Cousteau was already making plans for underwater scientific work when the war was over. He foresaw that free divers would become helpers of the oceanographers. An oceanographer is any type of scientist working at sea. He may be a physicist or a geologist, studying the earth beneath the sea, or a chemist studying the

water and the ocean bottom. Or he can be a biologist, working on the abundant forms of life in the water. "After the
war," Cousteau said, "I am going to have a special research
ship on which the divers and oceanographers can work together."

It was a distant dream. The war was not over yet. He and
Tailliez and Dumas helped their Navy rebuild. The French
fleet was almost gone, the navy yards in ruins and the water
full of German mines. The divers moved into a German
bomb shelter in the Toulon navy yard and put up a sign
"Undersea Research Group." Cousteau stopped sailors coming back to duty and said, "Join our outfit and see the
undersea world."

They had no orders from the admirals to start the Undersea Group. They just started it. The admirals did not notice
the tiny outfit, but they did wonder why equipment vanished from navy bases at night. The Undersea Group had
no other way to get what they needed. Soon they got two
diving vessels, the *V-P 8* and the *Élie Monnier.*

One day Cousteau was ordered to a dull desk job in Marseille. He hated to give up the Undersea Group. He was only
a lieutenant, but he went to see an admiral to try to stay
with diving. He showed his sunken ship movie and told how
the Undersea Research Group was clearing mines and doing
other useful chores. "The Undersea Research Group?" said
the admiral. "What is that? I never heard of it." Cousteau
confessed that it was not official. "The three of us started
it to help out." The admiral said, "Well, you young fellows
can't go around forming your own navies, you know. But
you seem to be doing good work and you have the right

spirit. You may go back to your group." After that, they didn't have to pick up equipment by moonlight.

The commandant at Toulon said to them, "We want to find out what kind of torpedoes the Germans used at the end of the war. There are some nearby, in a sunken U-boat." The divers went down and found that an explosion had opened up the back of the submarine. Dumas swam into the sub and cautiously made his way to the spare torpedo room. In the dark he saw torpedoes twice as long as he was. He made sure that the nose triggers were not set to go off. Using the built-in hoists and tracks with which the U-boat crew wheeled the torpedoes to the firing tubes, the Undersea Group removed them and hoisted them up. Dumas took a good pair of binoculars as his booty from the U-boat.

The divers were sent to bring up aerial bombs from the sea floor. In the hollow vane of each bomb there was an octopus, busy changing his color to blend in with the metal.

The Group installed decompression chambers. These thick steel chambers are charged up with compressed air in order to take a diver back into the same pressure he was in underwater. When a careless diver stays too long at serious depths, his body becomes saturated with nitrogen from the compressed air he breathes. After he surfaces the nitrogen forms terribly painful bubbles in veins and in his joints. The disease is called "the bends." To cure the bends the man is put back into pressure and they "bring him up" by slowly reducing the pressure in the air chamber. Civilian divers crippled with the bends were sent to the Group. They came out of the chamber singing and jumping and left their crutches as souvenirs.

CHAPTER V

La Calypso

THE UNDERSEA RESEARCH Group made several scientific voyages in its research ship, *Élie Monnier*. They sharpened Cousteau's dream of a ship of his own. She would cost hundreds of thousands of dollars, which he did not have. But he was confident he would find means, when he found the ship. In 1950, on the island of Malta, he found her, an unpainted former British minesweeper which was being used as a ferry between Malta and Gozzo Island.

Cousteau liked her ferryboat name, the *Calypso*, after the sea nymph in the *Odyssey*. She had a stout hull of seasoned Oregon pine and oak and two powerful General Motors Diesels: the *Calypso* had been built in the U.S.A. for the Royal Navy. The broad, low afterdeck designed for minesweeping would be fine for divers.

A wealthy friend offered to help Cousteau buy the *Calypso* and rebuild her at an Antibes shipyard. Cousteau took scientific leave from the Navy to begin his famous Calypso Oceanographic Expeditions. Explorers have a peculiar problem when they start out. They must have money to run expeditions and they must run expeditions before sponsors will give money. Cousteau did both things at once. His method consists of working twice as hard as anyone else and being in two places at the same time.

Since the first Calypso Expedition to the Red Sea in the winter of 1951-52, the ship has been at sea with scientists about nine months of each year. Cousteau conducts the "acrobatic" struggle for funds at the same time.

The *Calypso* has sailed two hundred thousand miles in the Atlantic and Indian Oceans, the Red Sea, Black Sea, Arabian Sea and Persian Gulf. Her skipper is Cousteau's first officer, Captain François Saôut, a skilled Breton seaman.

7. The Calypso, with whaling platform at the bow and tropical awnings spread.

Before he was thirteen years old Saôut had rounded Cape
Horn three times under square sails: in the French Navy,
he commanded just about everything from destroyers to
junks. The latter command was Captain Saôut's World War
II work. He ran the Japanese blockade for two years in a
junk, supplying underground fighters in Indo-China until
Japanese planes sank the boat under him.

If the *Calypso* should call at your port, Skipper Saôut
might very well invite you to come aboard and inspect the
research ship, as thousands have done in many ports. You
would come across a stern gangplank and have a look at the
drawbridge diving platform below on the transom. On a
diving station, the platform is let down just above the water
and the long diving ladder with handrails is fitted through
it, so the diving teams can travel efficiently between the
open afterdeck and the sea.

On the diving deck there is a jumbo hydraulic crane, with
two elbows that can delve delicately below decks, and
heave out Submarine Scooters and other devices and swing
them overside into the sea. On the diving deck there are also
several huge winches wound with miles of braided nylon
cable for lowering depth instruments. Nylon is weightless
underwater. On the diving deck is the divers' ready room,
containing diving gear, underwater cameras and repair
shop. Here are the compressed air outlets for filling Aqua-
Lungs. The compressors are below deck along with the
Submarine Scooters and other heavy gear.

Two-man cabins of scientists and expedition chiefs line
the outside passageways along the main deck. Cousteau's
double cabin includes a conference room. In the messroom

everyone aboard eats at common table: there are no distinctions of rank on the *Calypso*, and no uniforms. After dinner the crew uses the messroom for recreation. There are a phonograph, short-wave radio, chess sets, cards and stationery. Sometimes movies are shown at night on the diving deck.

The galley has a refrigerator that may be raided at all times. Also in the kitchen is a hidden passage through a trapdoor in the deck. It is the midships diving well, going down through the bottom of the ship. Cousteau designed it for diving in rough weather, when men going over the stern would be banged about in the waves. In the well you pass in and out of the sea immune to waves.

Since the *Calypso* is an undersea research ship, our in-

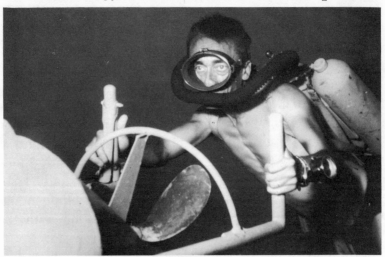

8. Captain Cousteau and the electric Submarine Scooter. Prop wash flows away under diver. He wears pressure gauge on left wrist.

spection tour should include her underwater part, which is just as familiar to her divers as the part above the surface. Get into your Aqua-Lung and let's go down the well. We are still inside the ship as we enter the sea. The waterline of the well is the same as the sea's. We go eight feet further down the ladder, open a hatch in the ship's bottom and step into the bright blue sea. Suspended in space beneath the ship, we look aft at her twin bronze screws and rudders and the lower rungs of the stern diving ladder. On the turning of the hull on either side of us are the sweeping stability keels. Nearby is a blister in the hull, a sonar transducer which fires ultra-sound pings at the sea floor and collects the echoes which tell how deep the water is and the shape of the floor.

We swim forward to an odd sight under the bow, a metal nose jutting forward eight feet underwater. There are windows in it. Inside there is a fellow lying on a mattress, talking on the phone. This is the *Calypso's* delightful underwater observation chamber, from which you can watch whales and porpoises frolicking ahead. When the ship sails among uncharted reefs, the observer sights ahead underwater and phones warnings to the bridge.

Returning aboard through the diving well, we unharness and take a shower in the crew bathroom near the bow. Nearby are the bakery and the marine biological laboratory. The V-shaped compartment furthest forward, the forepeak, is occupied by the paint locker. Sailors paint and chip continually to defeat salt corrosion.

Below deck, in the hot, oily engine room, the two shining Diesel motors thrust their propeller shafts back into the sea.

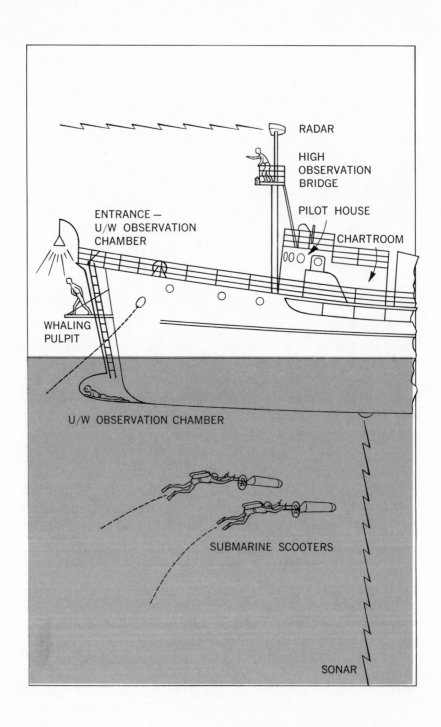

RADAR

HIGH
OBSERVATION
BRIDGE

PILOT HOUSE

ENTRANCE —
U/W OBSERVATION
CHAMBER

CHARTROOM

WHALING
PULPIT

U/W OBSERVATION CHAMBER

SUBMARINE SCOOTERS

SONAR

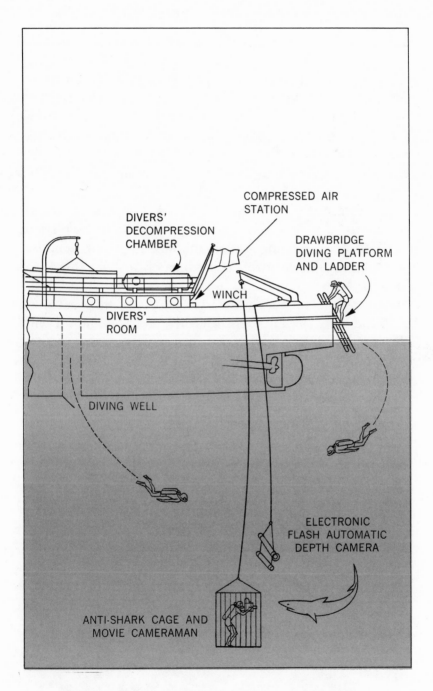

COMPRESSED AIR
STATION

DIVERS'
DECOMPRESSION
CHAMBER

DRAWBRIDGE
DIVING PLATFORM
AND LADDER

WINCH

DIVERS'
ROOM

DIVING WELL

ELECTRONIC
FLASH AUTOMATIC
DEPTH CAMERA

ANTI-SHARK CAGE AND
MOVIE CAMERAMAN

9. The legendary research ship, La Calypso, and her underwater
equipment, as she was in 1956. Cousteau changes ship around,
makes new additions or improvements every winter.

There are three powerful electric generators. For her size—360 tons—the *Calypso* probably uses as much electricity as any non-military ship afloat. The central systems control panel in the engine room seems to have a thousand dials and switches. Next forward are the machine and carpenter shops and an air-conditioned photo laboratory. Color films are processed on board.

The forecastle, below decks, is divided into neat two-man cabins for the crew. Nearby is the cold food locker and space to store camping and mountaineering equipment and souvenirs like "man-eating" Tridacna clam shells three feet long, or ancient jars found in the sea.

Now we go up the ladders two decks to the boat deck atop the divers' ready room. Here is the flag standard with the tricolor of France flying over a mahogany board with brass letters: CALYPSO TOULON. The yellow anti-shark cage is kept here and the two all-purpose launches, flat-bottomed aluminum boats with non-sinkable air chambers. With fifteen people aboard, a *Calypso* launch sits only eight inches in the water. The launches are also the ship's lifeboats and diving tenders.

On this white ship the main spots of color are the flag and a green insigne on the funnel, the naked nymph *Calypso* diving with a porpoise. The funnel is a dummy. Smoke is piped out the side near the waterline. The radioman sleeps in the funnel. Before the funnel is the superstructure, the brain center of the *Calypso*. The interior of the bridge is painted black to ease the helmsman's eyes. As he stands at the wheel, the gyrocompass is in front of him, engine-room telegraphs to right and left; hooded radar screen to the right; and over his left shoulder the automatic pilot. Behind him two steps lead down to the chartroom.

A chartroom usually has a table with maps stored beneath, a shelf of pilot books and a radio station. An undersea exploration ship needs a lot more than that. The *Calypso's* chartroom has three recording echo-sounders connected with blisters on the hull. It has a radio-telephone, a central mike for loud-speakers fore and aft and a wall phone connected to fifteen phones through the ship, including the one in the underwater chamber. There is an automatic course recorder, and an elaborate instrument for measuring and recording ocean swells. The *Calypso* can also make continuous recordings of surface currents while the ship is under way, with an instrument sensitive to the earth's magnetic field. Also in the intelligence center there is a well-equipped physics and chemistry laboratory to study the results of robot depth instruments such as reversing thermometers, Nansen bottles and bottom sampling gear.

Captain Saôut's room is next to the chartroom, so he can turn out on the bridge instantly in an emergency. There is also a ladder down to Cousteau's quarters.

Atop the superstructure is the flag deck with magnetic compass binnacle, gyrocompass repeater, flag locker and the divers' decompression chamber. Topping the ship is the high observation bridge, extending from side to side, and the radarscope. The flag deck is a fine place to sling your hammock on a hot tropical night. You may repose in great content, watching the high bridge swinging against the Southern Cross and the revolving radarscope trying to swallow the Dog Star.

CHAPTER VI

Exploring a Ship Sunk Before Christ Was Born

IN THE SUMMER of 1952, Cousteau and Dumas were conferring in the captain's quarters of the *Calypso* with a short, white-haired man named Professor Fernand Benoît. He is a famous archeologist, who has dug up Greek ruins going back to six centuries before Christ. The ship was sailing from Toulon toward Marseille on a new exciting mission: underwater archeology.

Dumas pointed out Grand Congloué Island on the chart. "Professor," he said, "we are coming to a spot where there seems to be an ancient wreck. I heard about it from a free-lance salvage diver, who was sent to us with the bends. The poor guy lost his toes, but we saved his life. He thanked us by telling his underwater secrets. The most interesting story was about Grand Congloué. He said that under the island there is a natural arch about a hundred feet down. If you swim west of the arch, you'll find a cliff full of lobsters."

46

Dumas continued, "I asked the crippled diver how far the lobsters were from the arch. He said, 'You'll come to a bunch of those old jars lying on the floor. The lobsters are right above them.'" Dumas waved his pencil. "You see, Professor, the jars are amphoras, and the diver didn't know their archeological importance. When you find a lot of amphoras on the floor, there is almost certain to be an ancient ship buried under them."

Baked clay amphoras were used in ancient times to carry water, olive oil, wine, wheat, iron and copper ore, seeds—anything that would flow through their five-inch necks. Ancient Greek and Roman ships were loaded with eight-gallon amphoras from the keel to high above the deck.

Cousteau said, "We're coming into Grand Congloué." They went on deck. The *Calypso* was passing through a channel as stark as the landscape of the moon. On one side was the mainland coast, a towering cliff of white limestone; and on the other was a chain of craggy islets without a sign of life. One was Grand Congloué, a stone layer cake, fallen on one side and rising 150 feet high. The *Calypso* anchored by the ghostly rock and Cousteau, Dumas and Benoît got into a launch.

Dumas rigged the aluminum diving ladder over the side of the launch and harnessed up. "The arch should be down about here," he said. He turned down in the blue water and found excellent underwater visibility, about seventy feet. Soon he saw the looming arch in its blanket of live coral and felt the thrill of discovery. Dumas is an ardent underwater archeologist. When he was thirteen years old, he uncovered a two-thousand-year-old grave on the seashore and began learning archeology—how to find buried objects and learn from them how people lived long ago.

He swam west from the arch along the steep island base. Soon he passed a few pairs of lobster horns, sticking out of crevices. There they were, but not half as many as the diver had dreamed. He turned down for the ancient jars, but saw nothing on the bank of hard fossil mud that the high island stood upon, half in the water, half in the air. He continued reeling across the floor, but saw no jars. His time ran out and he surfaced. Professor Benoît said, "Oh, well, let's go on to Maire Island. We're sure of an ancient wreck there."

Cousteau said, "I think I'll have a look at this spot, before we go on." He dived to the place Dumas' search had broken off, and continued swimming around the island, which is 450 feet long. He peered down into the mud, made up of the skeletons of trillions of tiny drifting animals that had died and rained down during the centuries. The mud was littered with rocks that had fallen from the island. Only trained eyes could tell amphoras from the rocks. The jars, too, would be covered with sponges and weeds. But Cousteau could see no graceful curves of amphoras. He swam far and deep, once dipping down to two hundred feet. He came to the end of his safety limit. It was a very strenuous dive. He turned toward the surface. When he reached 130 feet of depth, he came upon a mud shelf, half pocketed in the cliff. There, spreading far and wide, were hundreds of amphoras, tumbled about or with necks sticking up from the mud!

Among the big jars, Cousteau saw stacks of bowls and dishes. He had time only to scoop up three nested bowls

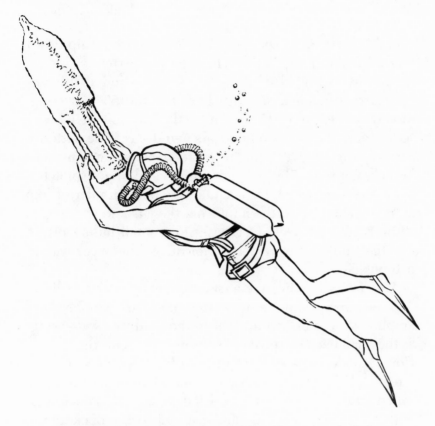

10. Archeological diver brings an ancient Roman amphora from a ship buried in the Mediterranean sea floor.

before he kicked for the launch high above.

Professor Benoît was impatiently looking into the water when he saw a hand holding three bowls rising from the sea. He grabbed the bowls and his face turned red with excitement. "They're third century B.C.," he shouted. "If there is a wreck, it will be the oldest seagoing ship ever found!" Cousteau climbed aboard and slumped in exhaustion.

"Don't worry, Professor," he said, "there's a big ship down there. I feel it in my bones. The signs are perfect."

The divers pelted down to see it. They found the amphoras spread on a sloping shelf 112 to 150 feet deep, directly under the vertical island wall. They lowered a wire basket and filled it with loose jars and dishes. The potteries came up covered with clinging oysters, sponges and mussels, branches of red and yellow gorgonians and bright splotches like fresh paint which were actually colonies of microscopic animals. They hosed the mud from the jars and an octopus slithered out on deck. Octopuses love small hiding places and the amphoras were perfect for them. The wreck was an octopus city.

The *Calypso* lowered a suction pipe and the divers "carved" away at the mud to free more jars. Hundreds of amphoras were buried upright in the mud, stacked exactly as they had been by stevedores twenty-two centuries before. Cousteau decided they would work two months on the wreck and bring up everything, buried ship and all. They sailed into Marseille with decks and passageways piled high with amphoras, and thousands rushed to the dock as the news spread of the great discovery.

As the *Calypso* continued the underwater dig, she was imperiled by anchoring so close to the rock. Several times winds rose suddenly and blew the ship toward the rocks. Cousteau decided it was too dangerous over the wreck. "Anyway," he said, "the *Calypso's* proper business is at sea, not hanging around unloading cargo that is twenty-two hundred years overdue." He continued, "The wreck is right under the island. Why not work from the rock?" Dumas said, "We don't have enough money to run the *Calypso* and this would mean planting a base on the island and keeping people here all the time." Cousteau said, "I have some ideas. I'd like you to go and explain the plan to Professor Benoît and see if he can get government funds." The government helped and so did the Marseille authorities. By now, the divers realized that bringing up the ancient ship would take longer than the two months they had originally set. (They didn't realize, however, that it would take six years.)

Cousteau invited General Mollé of the French Army to visit Grand Congloué. The general put on an Aqua-Lung for the first time in his life and swam 130 feet down into the excavation. He came up, exclaiming, "It's magnificent! Do you think she can be completely excavated?" Cousteau said, "Yes, sir, if we can get more help."

Three days later the *Calypso* landed a bunch of seasick army engineers on the rock. They blasted out a platform on the cliff, ten feet above the water, and installed a hand winch to lift wreck finds. In Marseille, Cousteau found some beat-up Nissen huts left by the U. S. Army, which was happy to let him have them if he would haul them away. The huts became a neat house for ten divers perched high on the island. The team planted an eighty-foot boom to carry a suction pipe out over the wreck and put an air compressor on the platform to power the suction pipe.

They named the new settlement Port Calypso, and hoisted their own green and white flag of the nymph and the porpoise. The Marseille Chamber of Commerce and businessmen adopted the islanders and sent them an elec-tric-light plant, a refrigerator, a two-way radio-telephone

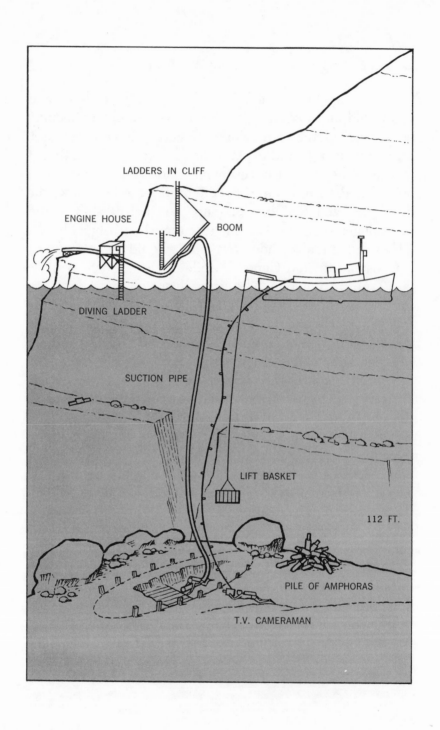

LADDERS IN CLIFF

ENGINE HOUSE

BOOM

DIVING LADDER

SUCTION PIPE

LIFT BASKET

112 FT.

PILE OF AMPHORAS

T.V. CAMERAMAN

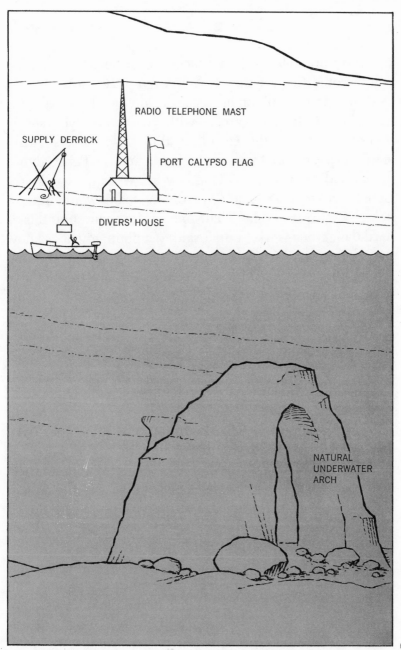

RADIO TELEPHONE MAST

SUPPLY DERRICK

PORT CALYPSO FLAG

DIVERS' HOUSE

NATURAL UNDERWATER ARCH

11. Port Calypso, island base of an underwater archeological operation on a freighter sunk about 205 B.C. Cousteau's divers have been working here since 1952.

and furniture. The National Geographic Society in Washington voted them money to help dig up the past.

Many excited volunteers asked to dive at Port Calypso. Captain Cousteau is careful with volunteers, who sometimes have more enthusiasm than ability. Volunteers hardly learn the job before they have to leave; and the Port Calypso divers had to stick to it. One day a lawyer named Pierre Labat said to Cousteau, "My diving team would like to help." Cousteau said, "Thank you, Monsieur, but this is hard dangerous work." Labat said, "Captain, my boys know their business. We are the French diving scouts, the first scouts in the world to become expert free divers. We have only older, experienced fellows."

Cousteau said, "Yes, scout training *is* serious." The diving scouts went out to the lonely rock and fished for history. Thousands of jars and dishes came up in the wire basket, along with hunks of the wooden hull, crew tools and sheets of lead with which the old ship had been entirely covered. The divers straddled the big suction pipe and carved deeper into the fossil mud. It was like riding a writhing anaconda. The pipe seemed like a living, shuddering monster. It sucked up mud, weeds, stones, fish—everything in its path. The divers were extremely careful not to get the mouth cupped against their bodies. The pipe would have stripped the flesh from their bones.

The divers labored strenuously to uncover the amphoras, pile them up beside the pit and load the lift basket when it came down. Someone had a brilliant labor-saving idea and took down an air hose. He filled an amphora with compressed air. It shot to the surface like a torpedo. But it was more trouble chasing jet jars around on the surface than loading them downstairs.

After several months' work the pit was deep and wide enough to reveal the ribs of the ancient argosy. The divers looked with emotion at a vessel unseen for nearly twenty-two hundred years.

Port Calypso was a frontier post, battling nature to survive. In the autumn came the cruel mistral, a whistling gale that sweeps off the mainland in this part of France, sometimes at ninety miles an hour. It is caused by sea-heated air rising after the land has already cooled in autumn. The cold air screams out to sea to take up the vacuum. The 1952 mistral hurled its might of wind and water at Port Calypso.

The waves heaved their backs under the engine house, knocking out planking and clutching at the big compressor. Spray blew over the peak of the island, flailing at the tin house. The divers came out in it to defend the engine house. They watched helplessly as the waves dragged the platform, the winch and air bottles down on top of the old wreck. The big boom swayed and its cables began to snap. Henri Goiran and Raymond Kientzy crawled eighty feet out on the whipping boom, disappearing from time to time in furious white waves. They secured the cables and ran back on the boom between waves. If they had been knocked off, there was not much chance of surviving. But they saved the boom and themselves.

The great mistral passed. The divers went down and hoisted their equipment. They built another platform several feet higher. Port Calypso fought five rounds with the annual storm and lost only one. The work went on with new rewards for their valor.

CHAPTER VII

The Search for Marcus Sestius

MANY AMPHORAS FROM the Port Calypso wreck had the mark "S.E.S." pressed into the rim, followed by an anchor symbol or a trident such as the Greek sea gods carried. As more of these marked jars came to Professor Benoît's museum, he wondered if S.E.S. might not stand for the man who had owned the sunken ship. An archeologist is really a detective of history, working on a big case—how we lived in ages past. The archeologist began tracing S.E.S. through other museums.

Early in 1953, Professor Benoît came to Cousteau with a face as flushed as the time he saw the hand come from the sea. "I have found Roman writings about a Marcus Sestius, a shipowner of the island of Delos in Greece," said the archeologist. "He lived in the third century B.C., the same period we think the amphoras and potteries were made. The Romans often shortened their names to make trademarks. Could S.E.S. be Marcus Sestius?"

Cousteau got as interested as the professor. He said,

"We're going to Greece this summer for depth photography. We'll stop at Delos and check your clue."

That summer I made my first cruise with the *Calypso*. We duly arrived at Delos, an island the color of a lion, all dried weeds and ruined white marble pillars and statues under an intense blue sky. Two thousand years before, the original statues, painted and gilded, stood along paths of flowers under high cedar trees. Greek families strolled these ways to the outdoor theater and to the waterfront, where high warehouses held the grain of Egypt, where swayed the masts of a hundred ships like the one buried at Port Calypso. All that was gone, except the battered and rain-cleansed remnants of marble. Delos had been raided and destroyed by pirates and the Roman Empire.

In 1953, only a dozen people lived on Delos, including French archeologists who had been digging for years to find what the place was like in the great days. Cousteau asked them, "Have you ever heard of Marcus Sestius?" It was a pretty hopeless riddle. We were looking for a man dead for 782,500 days. The chief archeologist said, "Yes, we have a record of Marcus Sestius. Professor Benoît has already asked us about him." The archeologist showed us a stone slab with words engraved in Greek. "This records that the Roman merchant, Marcus Sestius, was made a citizen of Delos late in the third century, B.C."

Cousteau said, "As a merchant he probably lived in the wealthy part of town." The archeologist said, "We know where that was. The rich merchants and shipowners lived behind the warehouses in lavish villas." He took us there. Many of the villas still had standing pillars, sections of walls, marble bathtubs, drains, empty niches where the household idols once stood and large sections of tile mosaic floors with beautiful pictures. One house was very interesting to us. It had a floor mosaic of porpoises and amphoras.

The *Calypso's* detectives scattered around the floor, studying each mosaic. Someone found an anchor symbol like the mark on the Port Calypso jars. Someone else called out, "Hey, look at this one!" It was the Port Calypso trident symbol, three prongs with "S" brackets between them, like this:

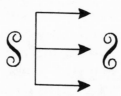

I had a sketchbook with me and was drawing the trident when it suggested something. I rearranged the trident, and showed it to Cousteau:

He turned to the chief archeologist and said, "Look at this. This might be Sestius' house." The scientist said, "It's ingenious, but it is not proof. This house never seems to have been lived in. We think it was unfinished." Cousteau said jokingly, "Maybe Sestius started the house, figuring he'd pay for it from the sale of his cargo in Marseille. The ship didn't come back and he was broke." Someone in the group carried this fanciful idea further: "Or maybe he went down with the ship." The archeologist smiled politely. "Amusing speculation," said he.

A diver who had been inspecting one of the mosaics said, "These little gray-black tiles are the same shape and color as some we found in the wreck." The archeologist said, "They are common in all these floors." The diver said, "Well, they aren't common on the sea bottom around Marseille, I can tell you." The scientist said, "These comparisons are suggestive. We should keep in touch as your excavation goes on. But, Messieurs, we have no proof of any kind that this house is connected with your ship."

However, some of us left Delos thinking we had come closer to the story of the ancient ship. Back at Port Calypso, the ship told its own tale as the divers sucked deeper with the pipe. There were two main types of amphoras, fat-bellied Greek ones and thinner Roman ones. The fat ones were stowed lower in the wreck, which meant they were loaded first; therefore the ship sailed from a Greek port. The Roman amphoras were on top, showing that the argosy next called at a port in Italy.

All the jars evidently contained wine for Marseille, which was then the Greek colony of Massilia. One day a jar came up with the cement stopper still in place, sealed with pine tar. The amphora contained a clear liquid and a bottom deposit of thick pink sludge, the remnant of red wine. Cousteau tasted it. His remark on sipping wine made more than two hundred years before Christ was born: "It was a poor vintage century." The wine had no taste of salt; the sea had not got into the jar in all the centuries.

Seven thousand amphoras and more than ten thousand

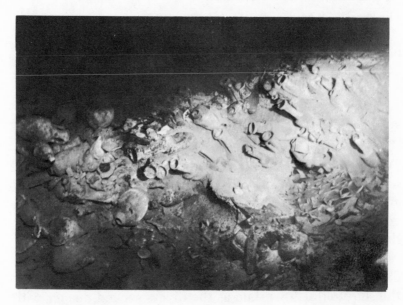

12. Side of excavation hole after six months shows thirty-foot panorama of amphoras, some still stacked as they were in the third century B.C. ship.

dishes, bowls, cups and flasks have so far been lifted from the wreck.

The dishes were stored in the afterhold. They are elegant blackware with red decorations and seals pressed into the clay. They are spread around outside the hull, indicating that the stern was stoved in and the dishes spilled out when the ship crashed. We began to visualize how the ancient accident happened.

The huge merchantman was nearing port with rich cargo and perhaps her crew grew careless thinking of shore leave after the long and perilous voyage. Or perhaps they were caught in a storm in the treacherous passage between the island and the mainland cliffs. Anyway, the ship crashed the eastern cape of Grand Congloué and went down rapidly. The stern quarters were either crushed in the collision or ripped open on a ledge during the fall, accounting for the scattered dishes.

Then the sea began her work of centuries to preserve the wreck. Nothing could eat away the clay jars and they became the homes of generations of sponges, clams, worms and weeds. Bacteria began to slowly consume the wooden superstructure, but a counter-process took place to bury and save the lower hull. It was the eternal snow of tiny skeletons of diatoms, dying and falling as mud to cover the ship. It buried bronze tree nails eighteen inches long that had been used to spike the hull planking to the ribs. It buried iron nails, hundreds of yards of lead plates and the smoke-blacked stone and earthenware cookpots the crew had used on the open afterdeck. The history of the ship is being studied by Professor Benoît and other fascinated archeologists who come from all over the world to study the finds in his museum. The cargo has overflowed the museum and is now filling up a nearby barn.

The divers measured and photographed the ship as they laid her bare. She was over a hundred feet long, very wide and deep-bellied, a giant of at least a thousand tons, three times as heavy as the *Calypso*. Sea historians had never dreamed that mariners sailed such colossal craft in classic times.

One day Dr. Jean Nivelleau, the Port Calypso physician, took his regular turn down on the pipe. He dived along the island wall, enjoying the beauty of the reef bouquets above the grave of the argosy. On a ledge sixty-five feet

down, he stopped to look at an oblong thing no one had
noticed before. It was the leaden stock, or upper crossbar,
of the ancient anchor. The rest had been wood, long since
rotted away. The doctor suddenly felt close to the men
who had lost their great ship and their lives in the old
tragedy. He could imagine them desperately throwing out
the anchor as they neared the fatal cape and he could
picture the ship falling through the water and the anchor
landing on the ledge. The lost freighter lay with her anchor
lodged above, trying to hook the sky.

Shy octopuses and other fish called the wreck their
home. There was an ugly scorpion fish, which hung around
for months, watching the divers carving up his real estate.
They were careful not to suck him into the pipe. At last,
when the old neighborhood was unrecognizable, the
scorpion sadly swam away.

The mud ran up the pipe and around the cape, where it
was discharged into the sea far enough away so as not to
cloud up the excavation. At the outlet there was a wire
basket to catch wreck finds. One day, by accident, a fragile
black cup got sucked in and came two hundred feet through
that furious pipe and crashed into the basket without breaking. A non-diver watched the basket, hoping to find coins.
The divers were amused by this romantic idea. One day
they fed some coins into the pipe. He grabbed them out
of the sluice basket and ran to the house, babbling about
treasure. A resting diver said, "Well, wash the mud off
them." When he did, he found three five-franc pieces dated
1950, worth less than two cents each. Another time the

13. Diver excavating ancient ship mound with suction pipe. He straddles pipe, holding on to handgrips.

divers sent the treasure hunter a live octopus through the pipe.

In 1953, Captain Cousteau tested his new underwater television chain at Port Calypso. The camera, in a steel barrel, sent pictures over a cable to a set in the *Calypso*. Jacques Ertaud took the camera down without knowing that there was a loud-speaker in the barrel, connected with a microphone in the ship. Ertaud was halfway down when a voice boomed through the sea, "Make the picture sharper, Jackie." He almost dropped the camera. With underwater TV, the archeologist could sit snug and dry on the *Calypso*, watching and directing the divers in the pit.

The months and years rolled by at Port Calypso, with diving day in and day out, in fair weather and gale. Life was hard, rugged and cold. Louis Malle, the young movie-maker who joined the *Calypso* team in 1954, was sent to Port Calypso to see if he could take it. Louis did. Afterward he said, "It was a school of men." There were gala days, too. One of the diving team was married on the island in a memorable ceremony in the sun. One New Year's Eve, Cousteau brought the divers' families and friends to the island. At midnight a celebrator yelled, "Who's going to get the first amphora of 1954!" A half dozen people suited up and plunged through the icy black water to grab jars.

The heavy mistral of 1955 forced them to stop diving. The citizens of Port Calypso sat around in their tin house as spray rattled against it. They listened on short wave to anxious ships battered in the gale and were happy to be on solid rock. One of the divers had to go to the outside toilet on the edge of the cliff. He thought he heard human cries mingling with the screaming wind.

He traced the cries to the cliff above the engine house, and looked over the edge. Down in the sea were three men in a tiny boat, struggling against the crashing breakers to get on the rock. The diver ran to the house for his friends.

Captain Cousteau's menfish swim out of the blue to greet a helmeted sponge diver. Hampered by the compressed air pipe between his legs and the safety line on his belt, the helmet man stumbles under his heavy weights. The free Aqua-Lungers soar around in space, weightless underwater. They breathe compressed air which automatically pressurizes them for any depth in their vertical range of 200 feet. Both helmet diver and free diver obey the same laws for breathing compressed air and are subject to the same time limits on dives. But the menfish can move anywhere and work more efficiently than the helmet man.

The underwater television camera ready to go into the sea. Too heavy to lift on deck, it will weigh nothing in the operator's hands underwater. Floodlights have 6,000-watt over-volted lamps.

Calypso camera team headed for the studio on the sea floor. They carry floodlights with power cables connected to the ship a hundred feet above.

Underwater observation chamber beneath the bow of the *Calypso* allows unique sights of whales and porpoises, sunken wrecks, dangerous reefs.

Diver penetrates the hold of the sunken S. S. *Thistlegorm,* a munitions ship bombed in 1941 on the Suez Gulf.

The first diver in the *Thistlegorm* scrapes coral from her bell, which becomes his souvenir.

Swimming through a snowstorm of tiny marine plants, a *Calypso* diver inspects the fore-deck wreckage on the bombed munitions ship.

Protected by the yellow anti-shark cage, cameramen film a ravaging blue shark horde attracted to a dead whale beneath the Indian Ocean.

The *Calypso's* electric Submarine Scooters haul explorers on long surveys of the bottom. Starter and accelerator are on the right hand grip. Diver steers by turning his body and fins as a rudder.

Albert Falco hitches a ride on the back of a giant sea turtle. The surprised reptile balked, paddled frantically, sank to the floor and swam to the surface without dislodging Falco.

Frédéric Dumas gains a thousand finny friends as he sows food scraps along beautiful Assumption Reef in the Indian Ocean.

Jean Delmas pets a big grouper, which adopted the *Calypso* divers under Assumption Reef.

Ulysses, the big grouper, blunders into the undersea studio, upsetting floodlights and scaring the other fish actors.

Ulysses, the friendly grouper, hates to see the divers leave the water. He swims up to keep them company near the surface as they hang onto the anchor chain to decompress.

They poured down the iron ladders set in the face of the cliff and pulled the three men to safety. The three men were Italian seamen.

A diver questioned them in Italian, while the others waited for the story. "Their ship, the *Donatello*, crashed on Riou and sank!" said the diver. Riou was the next island, as bare as Grand Congloué. "Their shipmates got ashore on Riou," said the interpreter.

Port Calypso swung into action. They radio-telephoned the *Calypso* in Marseille. Captain Saôut immediately cast off and sailed to the rescue in the roaring sea. The divers gave the heroic sailors dry clothes, wine and hot soup. Saôut took the *Calypso* into storm-wracked Riou and rescued the entire Italian crew.

As the storm died down, the Port Calypso team dived to the new wreck. She was a newly launched freighter loaded with casks of turpentine and wax cakes. The *Donatello* rested trim and upright on the floor, her fate proclaimed only by the collision hole and half-floating barrels spilled around her in the crash. Despite radar, sonar, electric steering and her powerful motors, she had crashed and sunk the same way as the clumsy Greek ship of twenty-two hundred years before.

CHAPTER VIII

Buried Alive a Mile Down

CAPTAIN COUSTEAU'S FIRST decade under the sea was the opening period of free diving. His team pressed ever deeper in the Aqua-Lung range, using cameras and floodlights to reveal the blaring colors of the blue reefs, colors never seen before by man or fish.

In 1947, he and four other members of the French Navy Undersea Research Group reached 297 feet, the known limit of compressed air diving. This carefully planned venture was done to study the strange effects of what they called "rapture of the deep." It is a kind of drunkenness which overcomes the will power of compressed air divers at two hundred or more feet down. You feel joyful, godlike and able to do anything. Rapture of the deep makes you sing and cavort, and you may end up by removing your mouthpiece, convinced you don't need air any more. Two men who swam deeper than three hundred feet have died of rapture. Scientists believe it is caused by a chemical effect of nitrogen on the brain centers. They call it "nitrogen

14. Stalwarts of the *Calypso* diving team confer before a winter plunge. Left to right: Albert Falco, André Laban, Armand Davso, Captain Cousteau, and Raymond Kientzy.

narcosis," but don't know much about it yet.

So the Aqua-Lung diver, for practical working purposes, is at the end of his range two hundred feet down. And below are greater wonders that Cousteau wanted to see. The beginning of his campaign to invade the lower depths came in 1947, when he called a conference at the Undersea Research Group at Toulon.

He said, "Professor Auguste Piccard is working on an undersea dirigible. He calls it the bathyscaphe, or deep-boat, and says it will take two men down twelve thousand feet." One of Cousteau's fellow officers said, "Doesn't seem possible. You would have too much weight of cable to lower

it that far. Beebe and Barton used the limit of steel cable
when they went to three thousand feet in the bathysphere."

Cousteau said, "The bathyscaphe isn't on a cable. She
goes down free and independent." The officer grinned and
said, "Well, anything'll sink, Jacques, but how is the professor going to come back up?" Cousteau replied, "The
bathyscaphe has an observation ball like Barton's but it
hangs from a metal balloon full of gasoline, which is lighter
than water. She has good buoyancy."

"Then how does she sink?" the officer asked. "You let
sea water into ballast tanks? I'd hate to depend on compressed air to blow out water tanks if I were two miles
down." Cousteau replied, "There is no water ballast. The
bathyscaphe has vertical tubes full of iron shot pellets,
held in place by electromagnets. You load enough shot to
send the boat down. If she sinks too rapidly, you press
a button shutting off the magnets for a bit. That drops
enough pellets to slow your sinking speed. And when you
want to climb to the surface, just trigger some more pellets
and up you go."

"What if you stop halfway down?" asked another officer.
"Nobody would be able to add weights to sink you." "In
that case," Cousteau answered, "you open valves to let a
little gas out of the balloon and you'll sink further." He
continued, glowing over the idea of going to great depths,
"The bathyscaphe has two thick plastic cone windows. You
could see things no one has ever seen before, when you turn
on the headlights down there in the dark. The Belgian
Government is backing the dirigible. She is called the
FNRS 2, the initials of the government scientific fund. Pic-

card is going to test her next summer off West Africa. I think we ought to join the expedition. We could take the *Élie Monnier* and navy weather ships to find the right conditions for the big dive." The Group agreed. It was an adventure much to their taste.

The first bathyscaphe expedition in 1948 failed to send men to the great depths. The balloon of *FNRS 2* was badly battered in surface waves and never had a chance. But Cousteau came back believing in the principle of the deep-boat. "What she needs is a seaworthy gas balloon, built like a submarine, so she can take surface weather," he said. He made a deal with the Belgians to take over the good pressure-proof observer's ball and the French Navy built a little submarine on top. This bathyscaphe, the *FNRS 3,* was finished in 1953. During construction, Professor Piccard left them and built a deep-boat called the *Trieste* in Italy. In her, he and his son Jacques went more than ten thousand feet down. But the *Trieste* has made few dives. The honors belong to the *FNRS 3,* which has now dived more than fifty times on scientific plans.

The French Navy's *FNRS 3* went 13,287 feet beneath the Atlantic Ocean in man's deepest descent, proving the faith of the Undersea Research Group. The master of the bathyscaphe was Commander Georges Houot and the engineer with him on the great dive was Lieutenant Pierre Willm.

There are plenty of stories about space travel and rockets to the moon, although no man has broken through the atmospheric skin of the earth. The bathyscaphe men, the deep men, have already penetrated far under the skin in stupendous pressure.

Captain Cousteau is photographic officer of the *FNRS* 3. The National Geographic Society paid for special electronic flash cameras to hang outside the ball. They were built by Dr. Harold Edgerton, the ingenious professor of electrical engineering at the Massachusetts Institute of Technology. One day he was Aqua-Lunging to check cameras on the deep-boat as she lay in her berth in the navy yard at Toulon. A man asked, "What do you expect to find down there?" Edgerton answered, "If I knew that, brother, I wouldn't bother trying." It was the philosophy of exploration in one crack: the bravery, skill and patience that some men have to discover the totally unknown.

Cousteau's second dive in the bathyscaphe was eventful. He came to the bathyscaphe with four cameras and a foot in a plaster cast. His son, Jean-Michel, had induced him to play tennis, and Cousteau had broken his foot. He entered the conning tower of the *FNRS* 3 and climbed down the entrance tube to the ball. Happily his leg cast went through the small door. Commander Houot bolted the hatch shut with a big wrench and phoned to the sailors on the conning tower, "Is the tow rope free?"

"Yes, Captain."

"Have the divers let down the guide chain?"

"Yes, Captain."

"Have they taken off all seven clamps to the electro-magnets?"

Cousteau said, "Yes, Georges, the divers are coming to the window and showing me the seven clamps."

Houot said, "If they forgot one clamp, we couldn't drop ballast and might get stuck down there." He stayed on the phone, calling off a list of thirty outside duties.

The last divers working outside held up fingers to show Cousteau the proper distance to focus his cameras on fish. Houot turned a valve which flooded the entrance tube, enough sea water to start the bathyscaphe down. They were headed for the bottom of the steep Toulon submarine canyon.

The deep-boat sank through the green silence that Aqua-Lungers know. The water turned blue, and soon they were falling below the range of divers, into darkness without a moon or stars, the unknown depths of our planet. One thousand feet down Cousteau switched on the outside searchlights. He said to Houot, "I see snow falling upward." The bathyscaphe was passing through flurries of tiny animals suspended in the sea. This zone of crowded little animals Houot and Cousteau referred to as "the soup." Edgerton and Cousteau had already made thirty thousand electronic flash photos in the soup with depth cameras financed by the National Geographic Society. Now Cousteau was seeing it with his own eyes.

Most of the snowflakes were crustaceans, the copepods. Others were larvas, tiny eggs, or transparent dots. Through the lucite port, Cousteau saw speeding arrow worms with inside shells visible through their transparent bodies. His searchlights caught silver hatchetfish so brilliant that they reflected the light like windows at sunset. Apparently the lights attracted many animals: clouds of shrimps drifted by, and small elegant jellyfish, or medusas, pulsated, showing their delicate blue or orange complexions against the black water.

The observer watched intricate colonies of animals called siphonophores, which are assembled in weird strings like the crochet work of a lunatic. Deadly tentacles dangled from these incredible communities of microscopic animals. The window revealed unknown elongated fish which hung head down in the sea, like yogis standing on their heads.

The bathyscaphe reached two thousand feet. Cousteau began seeing squids with torpedo heads and ten trailing tentacles. They dashed around outside and would stop suddenly and squirt glowing clouds of white ink. Cousteau thought of the great sperm whales sounding into this layer and snapping up squids and of the blue whale swallowing the shrimp hordes and straining them on the mustache inside its mouth.

"It's amazing," he said to Houot. "The soup gets thicker the deeper we go. Georges, what do you say we slow the dive a bit?" The skipper pressed the magnet release. Iron pellets fell out of the ballast tubes and pattered on the ball like summer rain. Houot switched on the magnet and the rain ceased. The *FNRS* 3 was now practically halted, a half mile down. "I'd like to see what it is like with all our lights out," said Cousteau. Houot obligingly cut the external searchlights and the lights in the ball.

They lay in utter darkness and silence. Cousteau stared through the port at an incredible milky way, at vast galaxies of minute glowing animals. Comets flashed among them. Some of the little creatures flared up green or bluish. A squid sped across the field like a rocket and left a phosphorescent cloud.

As the gasoline in the envelope above grew cooler, the

bathyscaphe became heavier and began to sink again. In a while Houot switched on the lights and glanced at the sonar tape. He said, "We are about two hundred feet from the canyon floor." Cousteau peered down into the blackness. He said, "I can see a faint glow of our drop-lights on the floor." Then the floor came into view. Five long sharks and a ray lay in the circle of light. They leaped up and away. The guide chain hanging from the bathyscaphe touched bottom and took away enough of her weight to stop the descent of the deep-boat. The landing was perfect. The *FNRS 3* rested just short of a mile down.

Cousteau studied the terrain outside. He said, "Georges, we are not at the bottom. We are on a little mud shelf on the canyon wall. Have a look." Houot peeked out. "It's a shelf all right," he agreed. Cousteau said, "Let's start the propellers and get off this ledge, hey?" Houot pressed the shot button for twenty seconds and the boat lifted five feet, ready to sail away.

Houot started the electric cruising motors on top of the bathyscaphe. They run in housings full of oil, which withstands the water pressure. As the *FNRS 3* pulled off the shelf, Cousteau saw a large hunk of mud falling off the ledge. It knocked off more clods as it fell into the canyon. Mud clouds boiled up from the black depths. The guide chain had apparently pulled the mud loose. The window became clouded over completely. It looked as though a sheet of yellow cardboard had been placed over the outside.

The bathyscaphe took a compass course for the other side of the canyon. For fifteen minutes she ran in and out of mud clouds, like an airplane passing through cumulous peaks. Then she passed through nothing but solid cloud for five minutes. Cousteau looked at the horizontal speedometer and said, "She's stopped dead. The mud specks on the window aren't moving." Houot said, "The props are still turning." He switched off the motors. "Do you think we have bumped into the canyon wall?" he said. Cousteau said, "Maybe. Let's wait for the mud to settle. What's for lunch?" Houot reached for his briefcase which he carries on vertical ocean voyages like a commuter on a train. It contained sandwiches and a bottle of red wine. The captain and the photographic officer of the bathyscaphe ate their lunch, tangling and untangling their long legs in a space not much bigger than a bathtub. They tried not to talk about their odd situation and spoil their digestions. Cousteau looked out the window for a baited hook he had hung a foot outside to attract fish to the camera. The hook was not in sight.

An hour passed and the mud remained thick as ever outside. Cousteau said, "Well, Georges, I guess it won't clear up for pictures today. Shall we go up?" Houot pressed the electromagnet release and dropped enough pellets to start climbing.

They watched the depth gauge and the vertical speedometer.

The hands of the dials did not move.

They were held fast a mile under the sea.

Neither man said anything. But on such occasions thoughts race quickly across the brain. Was it possible that, when she hit the canyon wall, the FNRS 3 had started another avalanche and was buried beneath it?

Houot and Cousteau knew they had more weights to

drop, perhaps enough to break out of a light covering of mud. The tubes still held several tons of pellets. They could drop the guide chain. Finally, they could press emergency buttons and jettison the heavy external batteries that ran the electric motors.

The deep-boat lay motionless. Silently, her crew thought of every possible reason why she would not rise. Then Houot said firmly, "She's cold. During the hour we've been here, the sea has cooled her off and made her heavier. We need to drop enough ballast to make up the difference." They calculated how much, and Houot held the release button down and timed the discharge with his stop watch. The seconds passed like hours.

"The specks are sliding down the window!" said Cousteau. "The vertical speedometer is moving. We're climbing, Georges!"

They ascended eight hundred feet before the bathyscaphe broke out of the mud cloud. In the region of the soup, the midnight water was full of living snow. The tiny animals seemed like old friends. Houot jubilantly repeated the "M" signal on his ultra-sound transmitter. "M" meant *Je Monte,* "I am climbing."

The sea flushed with weak daylight. They soared through the twilight zone into green and greener light. The ball began to rock. They were safely on the surface.

CHAPTER IX

The Wreck in the Gulf of Suez

COUSTEAU AND DUMAS leaned over the chart table, looking at a large-scale map of the Jubal Strait, where the Red Sea narrows toward the Suez Canal. The *Calypso* was a white chip in the spreading sea, under the orange and violet peaks of the Sinai Peninsula. It was so hot the calking compound melted between the deck planks.

Cousteau said, "There's a wreck under us somewhere. Here on the chart, she's shown in a hundred feet of water. I'll bet no diver has ever seen this one. Shall we try to find her?"

Dumas, always hungry for a virgin wreck, took the phone and asked the chief technician, André Laban, to come to the bridge. The *Calypso* stopped by a half-submerged coral reef and lowered a launch over the side. The boatswain put a metal barrel in the boat and took off for the the reef. He planted the barrel on the coral as a radar target, a fixed position around which the undersea search could evolve. The radarscope on the topmast began to turn, sending in-

15. The high observation bridge of the Calypso with radarscope
on top.

visible feelers through the air. Cousteau buried his face in the rubber hood around the radar screen. "The target shows up nice and bright," he said.

Laban drew the plotting sheet for the search. On transparent paper on top of the chart of the area, he made a wedge-shaped pattern of grids, radiating from the radar target in the reef. On an uncharted sea, this is the way underwater searchers fix their position at all times. The *Calypso* started to shuttle back and forth in the grid area, covering each section at a time.

She brought undersea feelers into play, to snag the wreck. Cousteau switched on the sonar recorder, or echo-sounder. Sonar draws continuous pictures of the bottom, giving the exact depth and contours. The hull blister, or transducer, fires a stream of high-frequency sound "pings" down to the floor, receives the echoing pings and translates them into a visual record in the chartroom. Since sound travels through water at 4,920 feet a second, the automatic sounder measured the split second it took the pings to bounce off this hundred-foot floor and fed the information into a stylus, or electric penpoint, which drew the profile of the floor on graduated graph paper which unrolled continuously in the window of the sonar set. The *Calypso's* Edo sounder is so sensitive that it will draw a dotted line going down if the cook throws an empty tin can over the side. On this flat shallow floor, a wreck standing perhaps fifty feet high would loom like a mountain on the sonar paper.

In addition to radar, plotting sheet and sonar, Dumas added human eyes to the search for the sunken ship. He went to the bow, opened a manhole and went down a ladder in an upright metal tube welded to the stem post. Eight feet below the waterline, he sprawled in the underwater observation chamber and began looking out for the wreck, ready to phone his observations to the bridge.

The *Calypso* sailed back and forth on the grid. The radar man, looking at the orange speck of the reef target, called off the ship's position and bearings for the helmsman and Laban, who marked the course they had covered on the plotting sheet. Now that the *Calypso's* eyes and senses were alert, Cousteau called for divers Albert Falco and Etienne Puig to harness up and be ready to jump from the moving ship as soon as she passed over the wreck. The two big brown men got down on the drawbridge diving platform, spit on their masks and rinsed them in water to prevent fogging on the dive.

The sea does not give up her secrets at your mere desire. For an hour, the *Calypso* shuttled to and fro, all her human and electronic capacities tensed as she swept and sniffed for the hidden ship. The radar man called his monotonous figures; Dumas phoned in from time to time, "Nothing to report"; and the sonar scroll inched slowly past the window, picturing a bottom as flat as Muroc Dry Lake. Patience is one of the main requirements of undersea exploration.

The sonar man said quietly, "Something is showing on the bottom." Cousteau looked in the window as the stylus sketched a steep rise from the floor. He called Dumas. "See anything now?" Dumas' voice came back. "There she is! I see her topmast!" Cousteau switched on the diving-deck speaker and yelled, "Falco and Puig. In you go!" The divers jumped feet first, holding their masks in place, and were covered in the swirling prop wash. The boatswain simultaneously threw in a small buoy to mark the spot. Skipper François Saôut eased the engine-room telegraphs and the *Calypso* slowed down, turned and went back to wait by the mark buoy.

The divers moved down in a stillness broken only by their slow, full intakes of breath, hissing from the regulator, and their exhalations, rippling out in merry bubbles. The water was clouded with algae, tiny sea plants. Eighty feet down there was no sign of the wreck. Then they saw something on the floor that looked like the backbone of a whale. It was the huge anchor chain of the sunken ship, covered with live coral. They hesitated; the ship had to be at the end of the chain. But right or left? They followed the chain along the floor and came to a huge anchor. They flipped over and swam in the other direction and came to where the chain slanted up. They followed it and saw a looming shadow, the forepeak of an enormous ship.

A diver has a feeling of sorrow when he first comes upon a ruined ship beneath the sea. There is excitement and romance in the idea of finding drowned wrecks, but the actual discovery brings a moment of sadness for the skilled designers, the hard-working shipwrights and the sailors who loved their ship: this ambitious creation of man fallen forever in the depths.

Falco and Puig paused, looking over the bow, and then swam slowly over coral-covered winches and deck guns blooming with animal colonies. Out of the fog of algae there came mysterious masses of crumpled metal, standing on railroad wheels, lashed to the maindeck. They were railroad tank cars that had been crushed by pressure. Yet the nearly naked divers were swimming easily in the same pressure, their chests fortified by compressed air.

Near the tank cars was the open main cargo hatch. The big hatch cover was missing, which was odd. Perhaps it floated off during the sinking. Falco gave himself a pull on the hatch coaming and glided thirty feet down into the hold. Puig followed his bubbles. The hold was full of army trucks and motorcycles. The divers played their flashlights around the hold and brought dazzling color pictures out of the blue mist—red and yellow coral fans and a brilliant circus of fish. A blue wrasse ducked under a truck. Veils of tiny pomfrets passed in the hold. Lazy groupers loitered on the steel plates, changing their colors to fit the background. Man's ruin had become a fish hotel.

The divers swam past the superstructure and came upon a chaos of twisted metal. The wreckage had lost the appearance of a ship. It was now clear that the ship had exploded. She was a large freighter filled with military equipment. She had been sunk either by a torpedo or an aerial bomb.

Men must have died in the explosion. Falco and Puig found no trace of them except a decaying leather sea boot. Bodies are consumed by crustaceans and bacteria in a few weeks under the sea.

The divers wondered what was the name of the freighter. On the charts, she had simply been marked "wreck." But the name lives forever on the ship's bronze bell, which is the rightful trophy of the first divers in a wreck. They swam up the superstructure and found the bell covered with rosy coral. The name was buried. Falco drew his knife and struck the bell. Simultaneously the bell sent a clear chime through the sea and a little blue fish leaped out.

Now they had only three minutes left in the wreck depth, not enough time to cut away the bell. They were forced to surface without the prize.

CHAPTER X

The Treasure of the Thistlegorm

THE NEXT MORNING Falco and Dumas dived to take the bell. As they worked, a vast dark shape moved toward them off the ship's rail. Dumas and Falco have had long experience in the water and do not scare cheaply, but the first glimpse of this thing sent them scuttling down into the hold.

They peered out as it passed. The thing was a fish with an upright slab of a body about three feet thick. It was nine feet high and twelve feet long. It was like a living wall. It was denim blue with vertical black stripes thick as tree trunks. It had a high bulging forehead, a jutting, brutal, toothy mouth and transparent fluttering fins as big as palm fronds. The great fish turned about ponderously at the bow and paraded back alongside the wreck, rolling its inboard eye at Dumas and Falco as it passed them. They climbed out of the hatch and hung in mid-water, staring in bare wonder. The world of men and fish had turned inside out. Men had been shrunk to pet-size by this fish.

16. Falco reports the great wrasse of the Thistlegorm to Cousteau.

On the diving deck the timekeeper was growing anxious over their bubbles, which were still breaking in big blobs on the surface, showing that they were still deep. Their time was running out. Then the bubbles became smaller. The timekeeper said, "They're coming up." Falco and Dumas arrived quickly, slipped their mouthpieces and began to yell about the gigantic fish.

Cousteau reached down to the diving platform and relieved the weight of Dumas' air bottles as he came up the ladder. "A whale?" asked Cousteau. "Absolutely not," said Dumas. Cousteau said, "Maybe a whale shark. They get to be twelve feet long." Falco said, "No, sir, this was not a whale shark."

A sailor said, "How did you know he was nine feet high and twelve feet long? Did he stand still while you measured him?" Falco was annoyed at being doubted. He yelled, "He passed a truck on deck, and he was as big as the truck." The sailor grinned. "Aha, a truckfish!" said he. "Falco saw a truckfish." Cousteau gave the sailor a sharp look and said, "Laban, jump down and see if you can film him." Laban and his companion returned in fifteen minutes with unsmiling faces.

"The visibility was too poor to film him," said Laban. The skeptical sailor said, "You *saw* the truckfish?" Laban said, "We sure did. He is as big as they said he was." The next team did not see the monstrous fish at all. Dumas dived again and went to work on the bell, looking for the big fish out of the corner of his eye. It did not appear. He knocked off the ruddy coral from the bell and scraped down to the letters:

SS THISTLEGORM GLASGOW

That night the divers who had seen the big fish were reluctant to talk about it. They laughed nervously, beginning to doubt their own eyes. Cousteau believed his four divers and took them aside from their laughing shipmates. Dumas said, "It is almost square, Jacques. Something like seeing a manta swimming on its side. But it is absolutely a fish. It reminds you of some reef fish, but the proportions and the size don't fit anything I've ever seen." Laban said, "It probably lives in the wreck and doesn't like us coming down and blowing bubbles in its house."

The "truckfish" sensation died down somewhat as the diving teams began commuting between the two ships fifty feet apart. As they explored the *Thistlegorm* no more

was seen of the great fish. On the third day cameraman
Louis Malle and Dumas were filming around the bridge.
Malle was still keeping an eye out for the big fish. Suddenly
he saw it materialize from the egg-filled mists. It stared at
the divers, and, as though disappointed to see these bubble-
blowing creatures still camped in its house, the big fish
faded into the sea. Malle's description tallied exactly with
that of the previous witnesses.

The free divers slithered inside the wreck, through any
spaces that would pass a man. Their mobility was much
greater than that of helmet divers, who usually work on
wrecks. After lengthy preparations and the help of his as-
sistants, the helmet man is lowered on his air pipe and safety
line. He must carefully mind the valves that control the in-
flation of his suit in various pressures. On the bottom he is
virtually a prisoner of his lines and his heavy boots, helmet
and breast weight. As he is hauled up, the helmet diver's
most dangerous zone is the top thirty-three feet, where the
pressure change is the most, from two atmospheres to one.
If he does not valve off enough air, his suit can balloon and
zoom him to the surface with his arms helplessly extended
by the swollen suit.

The Aqua-Lungers flew through the *Thistlegorm* like the
fish that lived in her. Dumas flipped into the hold and
climbed into the driver's seat of a truck. He pressed the
starter but was unable to run over a single fish. The divers
picked pearl oysters from anti-aircraft guns and reached
for bottles floating against the ceiling. Along the passageways they strolled with striped porgies and blue angelfish
with yellow maps of Madagascar on their sides. Blue- and

black-striped wrasses up to three feet long also lived in the *Thistlegorm*. They are vegetarians that live in reefs and wrecks.

Luis Marden, the National Geographic Society photographer, was making color flash shots in the wreck when all of a sudden he saw the "truckfish." It hung off at a distance. Marden swam toward it, trying to get a photo, but the fish turned tail and vanished.

The *Calypso* sailed away to another location and returned two months later. Cousteau briefed the divers before work began. "The big fish may have come back to live in the wreck. We may have a chance to film him, so take it easy and try not to scare him." He and Laban waited for the midday light and went down with the movie camera.

As they reached the main deck, Laban clutched Cousteau's arm and pointed. There was the truckfish! It was gliding along the rail. Cousteau turned on the camera and tracked it, hoping that something could be filmed through the speck-filled water. And as he turned the camera, he identified the fish.

It was a hump-headed wrasse. The species is a placid vegetarian one. The divers had seen them nibbling on many a reef. The wreck of the *Thistlegorm* was full of wrasses. But the reason why they had never been able to connect the giant with the wrasses was its colossal size. *No one had ever seen a wrasse more than three feet long.* This great humphead was thirty times the size of the biggest wrasse ever seen before.

Cousteau surfaced and waited for the end of the film to be developed to see if he had the truckfish. There was nothing on the film but blue water and white specks. Seven men had seen the zoological sensation, but he would not sit for a picture. The colossal hump-head reminded them of a strange fact about the undersea world, that some fish never stop growing. If they live long enough, they attain the fantastic dimensions of the fabulous truckfish of the *Thistlegorm*. As diving continued, they never saw the great wrasse again.

One day Dumas and Malle swam into the bridge house, past the coral-covered helm, compass and engine-room telegraphs. They carefully avoided entangling themselves in pipes and wires shaken loose in the explosion. Dumas unhinged the door to the captain's cabin with his knife and his blue flippers vanished inside. He played his flashlight on scaling walls, a crusted radiator and a red scorpion fish standing upside down on the wall. The scorpion sprang away and Dumas tracked it with his torch. The beam lighted on something that made Dumas forget the game with the scorpion.

His light shone on the captain's safe. Dumas thought excitedly, *The ship went down so suddenly, nobody would have had time to remove anything from the safe. Here is the treasure of the* Thistlegorm!

He beat it to the surface and reported the find. Gold fever broke out on the *Calypso*. "The safe is small. It would be easy to lift it up," said Dumas. Cousteau listened on the edge of the crowd. He said, "It would be a waste of time. There can't be anything valuable in the safe. In wartime no captain is allowed to carry money that the enemy could capture. The company gives him letters of credit to cash in friendly ports." Cousteau saw that the men were very disappointed. "Do you still want the safe?" he said.

"You bet!"

"Let's go!"

"All right," said Cousteau. "But remember the safe still belongs to the steamship company. We will have to ask them for a salvage share and then divide it equally among all of us." Everybody agreed this was a fair and square way to handle treasure. Cousteau said to Henri Plé, an older diver who was respected by all, "Uncle Henri, you be the wreckmaster and see that everything is done fairly."

Divers carried down the end of a steel cable and fastened it to the safe. The deck winch gave a burst of power and the divers guided the safe out of the cabin and followed it to the *Calypso*. Second engineer René Robino chiseled off the door of the safe as everyone crowded around, yearning to see the treasure. Uncle Henri reached in and pulled out a big wad of soggy paper. He peeled away the outside layers and held up rolls of sonar charts, records from unknown seas, that the captain of the *Thistlegorm* had stuck in the safe. The treasure seekers giggled nervously at the worthless charts.

Plé said, "Stand by! There's a little drawer here on top." He jerked it out and found a rotten leather wallet. By this time he had a football huddle around him. He pulled out a sheaf of wet papers and separated them. "The captain's membership cards," said the wreckmaster, "and receipts for port dues."

"There's another part to the wallet!" said Henri Goiran. "Open it!" Uncle Henri delved and came up with some paper money. The treasure hunters yelped for joy. Uncle Henri smoothed out the bills on deck. They consisted of a Canadian two-dollar bill and an English pound note worth $2.80. There was nothing more in the safe. The loot of the *Thistlegorm* amounted to less than five dollars. That meant that, if the owners of the ship granted them the usual 50 per cent salvage share, each victorious treasure hunter would get less than a dime.

Cousteau said, "Okay, Uncle, when we get to Suez, send the money to Scotland and apply for our share." The wreckmaster smoothed out the two bills to dry overnight. In the morning, they were crumbled to bits, the dust of the treasure-hunter's dream.

CHAPTER XI

Hunting Undersea Oil on the Pirate Coast

THE *CALYPSO* SPED along in the azure Arabian Sea, bound for the Persian Gulf to explore for oil beneath the sea floor. On the high observation bridge stood three men dressed in shorts and Arab turbans. *Calypso* divers like to wear the headdresses of the countries they visit. The lookouts gazed over the dancing waves for any sights of interest. The white ship was alone in the world. Suddenly watchers yelled down to the pilot house, "Reef ahead! Waves breaking over a submerged reef. Dead ahead." Captain Cousteau was surprised. There were no reefs on his chart of this open sea.

Cousteau climbed to the high bridge with a pair of glasses. "It's not a reef," he said. "It's a line of porpoises splashing the water." The ship came up to the porpoises. For miles on either side they leaped out of the water, thousands upon thousands of them. Porpoises are not fish, but air-breathing, warm-blooded mammals that nurse their young. They are intelligent, fun-loving creatures with grinning lips. Sailors often see them come to race the ship, making fun of her. A porpoise can outspeed the fastest ship.

No one on the *Calypso* had ever seen so many. Nor had we ever seen such jumps. Eight-foot porpoises were shooting twelve feet out of the water and falling back with high splashes. They surrounded the research ship, wheeling and leaping. From the underwater observation chamber we watched them flirting with the *Calypso*. They spurted ahead with a flick of their flat tails. In their mighty jumps they would twist around in the air and fall in awkward belly-floppers to make a bigger splash. They got into our wake waves and used them as springboards to vault even higher. It was some kind of porpoise holiday, all fun and games. After two hours of showing off, they formed their line again and turned on the speed. The living reef marched away from our bow, out of sight over the blue rim of the Arabian Sea.

We turned into the Persian Gulf to visit the hottest place on earth. This is the Elphinstone Inlet, a long twisting channel surrounded by the burning cliffs of the Masandam Peninsula. It was not the hottest time of the year so we stood it pretty well. At the furthest point of the inlet we found a village of mud huts, containing a hundred poor Arabs. They fish in the winter and when the terrible summer comes, they climb a four-thousand-foot mountain above the village and work on date farms in an oasis. They were netting tiny fish and drying them on the beach. The dried fish go to the island of Bahrein where they are fed to

Anglo-Iranian Oil Co., London

17. While exploring for oil beneath the Persian Gulf, Captain Cousteau worked long hours in the chartroom.

cows; there isn't much grass on Bahrein so the cows have learned to like fish.

The Pirate Coast, where we went to find undersea oil, got its name from sea robbers who used to come out and attack ships. The pirates are now pretty much satisfied with oil money, but there are still some raids in these waters. The pirates are thin, tough fellows with eyeliashes tattooed on their eyelids.

How do you find oil under the sea floor? Oil is usually in hollow underground domes or sand layers, which give you the first clue. Domes are located by a big bell-shaped instrument called a gravity meter. The *Calypso's* gravity meter was on a track on deck, so that it could be run out over the side and lowered to the bottom. It had electric cables running up to a control room on deck. When the meter touched bottom it automatically set itself dead level on the floor. Then it started measuring the gravity of the earth at that point and sending the information to the ship. If the gravity was slightly different than it should be, it could mean an oil dome beneath the bottom.

Next we dropped the coring bomb, a half ton of solid steel with a hard coring pipe in the nose. The pipe drives into the floor and comes up with a sample of rock. Captain Saôut rigged the coring bomb from the crane and swung it over the stern. It hung by a rope and loose steel cable. He cut the rope and the monster plunked into the water. He started the winch and the bomb came back up on the steel cable. "Hey," said Saôut, "the coring pipe is missing!" Falco laughed and said, "Maybe a shark bit it off." The divers disliked the bomb—they said they could get rock samples themselves.

Henri Goiran and Dumas dived for the missing pipe. Forty feet down they came to a bright, flat, sandy floor. There lay the coring pipe, bent into a "Z" shape. A crowd of fish were looking at the twisted pipe. How could it bend in sand? The divers dug with their hands. Underneath there was a bed of solid rock. They brought up the ruined pipe, rather enjoying the defeat of the bomb.

"Jacques," said Dumas, "we can get rock samples with a compressed air drill"—the noisy tool used to dig up streets. Dumas rigged the drill and went down. He stuck the point into the rock and turned it on. He didn't make a dent in the rock. Instead, the jabbing drill just bounced on the floor.

He came up, complaining how hard the rock was. The situation was getting serious. A costly expedition couldn't even get a chip of rock to test.

Falco said, "Let Kientzy and me have a try." The two strong divers went down with a chisel and sledge hammer. They swept away the sand with their foot fins until they found a crack in the rock bottom. Falco held the chisel in the crack and Kientzy swung the hammer. It arched over his head in slow motion and rang on the chisel. They pounded away for quite a while before some pieces of rock came loose. The chief geologist received them with delight. He took them to his lab and emerged grinning. He handed Cousteau a jeweler's magnifying monocle and said, "Look at this tiny sea shell in the rock! That's nummulite. When you see that, it's a pretty fair sign of oil."

Working from radar targets on shore, a marine surveyor

fixed the *Calypso's* position with great accuracy as she
proceeded from one place to another, lowering the gravi-
meter and sending divers for rock samples. Usually the
human zoo, or anti-shark cage, was placed near the divers,
as a refuge if sharks got too nosy. The cage was useless
against the biggest danger of the Persian Gulf, poisonous
sea snakes that could have slithered between the bars with
ease. Kientzy, who hated the snakes, would try to pound
them into the floor with his hammer. The snakes didn't bite
anybody.

The divers completed four hundred oil stations in two
months. We sailed away with precise locations of where
oil might be found, when the drilling barges came later.

CHAPTER XII

Isle of Paradise

THE *CALYPSO* SAILED south for ten days on the calm Indian Ocean without sighting land. Only once did we see another ship on this loneliest of oceans. But every day we saw flying fish. They are actually gliding fish. When eluding enemies, they beat their tails furiously until they have enough power for take-off, then set their pectoral fins like wings and soar low and fast as far as five hundred feet.

At last the weary watchers on the high bridge saw a line of green dots rise from the sea ahead—the tops of coconut palms. It was Aldabra, an island thirty miles long built entirely of coral skeletons. Twelve men and two dogs rushed into the first launch going ashore. When we came to the fringing reef, the coral fence around the island, we found a break in the reef. We jumped into the water, lifted the Evinrude propeller and pushed the boat through the gate.

The beach was sugar white. In the draining tidal flats between the reef and the beach, hundreds of black egrets and white egrets dipped their bills in puddles for worms and little fish. The egrets paid no attention to us. Aldabra Atoll is one of the rarest places on earth, an ocean wildlife preserve where man has never killed and despoiled.

We plunged inland on our own deserted island, walking on scented pine needles and powdery sand in the shade of the palms. Red coconut crabs basked in the sun; the bushes bent under roosting sea birds—gannets and big white booby chicks. Frigate birds, the best aviators in the tropical sky, floated above on eight-foot wingspreads. We came to a cemetery with faded wooden crosses, with Asian, African and European names on the leaning boards. Once there was a copra plantation on Aldabra, where people dried white coconut meat to make oil and soap.

Crossing a grassy plot, Maurice Léandri halted the march. "What's that?" he said, pointing. A boulder was moving across the grass. It was a giant land turtle. Aldabra is one of the two places on earth where they still live. Soon turtles were all around us, some with shells two feet high and three feet long. They were cropping the grass, neat as lawn mowers. There are probably a half million giant turtles on the island. The divers climbed on their backs and rode around.

We came to the decayed wooden and coral houses of the old plantation, and broken-down boat sheds roofed with palm fronds. The bleached bones of sea turtles lay around the boatsheds. A mild voice said, "*Bon jour, Messieurs.*" We looked around for the speaker. Out of the pines came a small barefooted man in shorts. He had long gray hair and blue eyes and he was wearing a sun helmet painted silver. He said, "I am Georges Hoareau, governor of the island." We were a bit shocked that our "deserted island" came complete with a governor. "Welcome to Aldabra," said he. "I didn't know you were coming. My radio went out of order some years ago. Have there been any wars lately?"

The governor conducted us to his mansion, an unpainted wooden bungalow on pilings with a huge concrete rain catch basin in front. On the veranda stood a smiling Negro lady six feet tall, wearing a dress of many colors. "This is Angelina, my secretary of welfare," said the governor. I asked, "How many people live here?" Hoareau replied, "We are seven, Monsieur."

He told us how seven people came to live in Paradise. Aldabra is controlled from the British Seychelles Islands, eight hundred miles away. The government had sent Hoareau and his people as caretakers of the atoll. Once a year— some years—a supply boat came with tobacco, sugar, tea and flour. But if the boat didn't come, the islanders lived happily on sea turtles, wild celery, tomatoes, coconuts, chickens, eggs, pigs and goat milk.

The governor gave us two houses on the beach and Angelina cooked the food we brought with us. For a month we stayed on the atoll, while our scientists studied the natural history of the fortunate isle. The *Calypso* prowled around the reef, exploring undersea Aldabra. The divers took turns coming ashore for a rest and Angelina's meals. She could make a handful of twigs cook like a big electricity bill.

Cousteau came to the mansion one night and said, "Tomorrow we'll have a look at the lagoon." The interior of Aldabra is a vast lagoon bigger than Manhattan Island.

There are three narrow channels to the sea. They are not wide enough to ease the water in and out with the tides; it rushes in and out at great speed.

The launch carrying the lagoon expedition started through Johnny Channel. The tide was coming out at six or seven knots an hour. Louis Malle dropped into the current with a movie camera and let himself be carried out to sea. He made "trucking shots" in which the camera moves toward and past subjects. Trucking shots cost a fortune to make in a studio. Shooting along in the tide, Louis got his free, except for cuts and bruises when he was thrown against the coral walls.

The great lagoon mostly consists of flats that drain at low tide. There is a network of deep pools and channels and wide mangrove jungles. Cousteau took the launch among the standing roots of the mangrove trees. Far into the Venetian alleys of the water forest the launch glided; we felt almost as far from the world as in a deep dive in the sea. In the green quiet we looked into the transparent water at dazzling coral heads. When it became too shallow, we lifted the outboard and poled further in the maze. This was a jungle in which air and sea animals mingled in the roots of trees. Gannets perched on the arching roots, a few inches above the fins of dozing sharks. Drooping leaves almost brushed the dorsal banners of angelfish. Tropical nature in this wild lagoon came as close together as pages stitched in a picture book.

Here and there we came upon colossal gray pillars of mushroom coral standing from the water. Although Aldabra was formed entirely by coral, there seems to have been an upthrust of the sea floor in past ages to raise the eroded towers of dead coral. They are twenty feet higher than the sea. The lagoon is a strangely beautiful and unique place.

Aldabra has no weather. It is practically on the Equator, but has a warm, temperate climate the year round. In the monsoon season, little rain clouds buzz over from India like blimps, leaving a patter of rain as brief as the sound of a passing plane. We took showers in the funny rains and watched the clouds puffing toward Africa, leaving double-rainbows. One night, after dinner, we were all lounging on the snowy beach in the starlight, watching the lights of the *Calypso* riding beyond the barrier reef. Suddenly the full moon leaped up behind us and caught one of the fleeing rainheads. A white lunar rainbow formed over the ship. The spectral arch was very distinct; when we squinted our eyes, we saw faint colors in it. None of us had ever heard of lunar rainbows, let alone seen one.

CHAPTER XIII

An Incident in the War of Men Against Sharks

"WHALES!" DUMAS SHOUTED from the high bridge. "They look like sperm whales." We were sailing the equatorial Indian Ocean, six hundred miles east of Africa. Cousteau turned toward the whales. He will abandon course any time to watch them. Dumas' shouts became more excited. "It's incredible! Did you see that?" The rest of us saw a high waterspout on the horizon. "A big whale jumped clear out of the water!" yelled Dumas. Only Dumas and Falco saw a sixty-foot sperm whale breach into the sky and fall in the geyser of spray.

The *Calypso* drew up to the whales, which were swimming along slowly, dipping in shallow dives, and blowing their slanty, misty spouts from their left blowholes. They were not scared of the ship. We counted nine whales loafing along just ahead of us. Our crew crowded the bow and bridge, yelling and pointing in wonder. It seemed to be a

18. Baby sperm whale shackled to the Calypso. Anti-shark cage on right, movie cameraman out on spar at left.

whale tribe with a bull, several cows and two calves. The little whales, about twenty feet long, were probably only two or three months old.

The area we were crossing was called the Seychelles Grounds by old-time whaling-ship men, who were supposed to have exterminated sperm whales in these waters. Most surviving whales sought refuge in the Antarctic. Yet here were full-grown whales swimming along as if they owned the Seychelles Grounds.

The *Calypso* pushed into the formation. From the underwater chamber we watched tail flukes twelve feet wide flapping up and down, as the gigantic animals lazed through the clear sea. From the bow we saw their pale bulks shimmering under the surface and their backs hump out of the water. Their spouts became rainbows and drifted over us.

One of the whales turned across our path and there was a shuddering crash as the *Calypso* bumped fifty tons of animal. Things clattered throughout the ship and the glass in the chartroom door fell in splinters. The whale seemed to have its wind knocked out. It could not dive or swim as fast as the others. Two whales fell back and gathered to its sides, shouldering it along.

Cousteau ran to the Edo sounder. Over the headphones he heard the voice of the mighty whale, a shrill pip like a mouse squeak. The squeaks sounded through the sea, a cry of distress. Then, from all corners of the watery world, came whales to their member in trouble.

Soon we had twenty-seven whales marching around the injured one. The two babies stumbled along as though learning to walk. One of them drifted back toward us. The watchers up front yelled, "Look out!" but before Cousteau could dodge, there came another crash. Engine-room bells rang on the bridge. It was René Robino, the second engineer, reporting, "My port engine is stopped." Cousteau phoned back, "I think we hit a whale. Start her up again." Robino got the engine started.

Behind us the water was stained red. The sharp propeller blades had cut deep wounds across the little whale's back. It struggled to catch up with the others, and for a time stayed with them.

Another whale drifted back to us. It was the colossal bull, the monarch of the tribe. He came alongside and rose straight up from the sea, until two thirds of his length was out of the water. He seemed to stand on his tail for a long moment, and we saw his eye turning and glaring at us. He fell back in the water, rocking the *Calypso*. Undoubtedly he was the one that had leaped into the air, probably to get a better look at the approaching ship. The big bull started across our bows, swimming rapidly. He evaded the onrushing underwater chamber and proceded swiftly away. Now the entire herd took up determined ranks behind him and hastened away too fast for us to follow. We were convinced that he had decided the baby could not be saved and he had ordered his family to abandon it and save themselves.

The injured whale was growing weaker. Saôut took up a harpoon of mercy and slid down to the platform beneath the bow. As he hurled the harpoon, the retreating whale tribe threw up their flukes and sounded to the depths of the sea.

The harpoon was fast in the whale. Saôut went up the rope to the deck and ran along the top of the port rail the whole length of the ship, holding on to nothing but a line to a struggling whale. Below him sinister shapes had already appeared—big gray sharks and blue sharks, shimmering just beneath the surface. Sailors got nooses over the whale's flukes and hauled the tail against the stern. Dumas took his rifle and put the whale out of its misery with one shot.

A dozen sharks circled the whale. They cautiously stayed thirty feet away from it. Cousteau saw a chance to film a sight no man had seen who lived to tell the tale—the underwater attack of a shark horde. "Break out the cage," he called. The yellow anti-shark cage was hoisted over the stern and held against the ship for Cousteau and Laban. They entered with Aqua-Lungs and a movie camera. The

19. Cameramen are lowered in the "human zoo" to film sharks in Indian Ocean.

crane swung the human zoo away from the ship and the two divers sank into the sea. The cage hung from a half-inch cable. Of course, it was strong enough, but everyone looked at the slender cable going into the water. If it broke, the cage would fall three miles. Cousteau and Laban would have to escape before the cage reached fatal depths, less than three hundred feet down. Then they would have to make their way to the ship through the hungry sharks.

The cage went down twelve feet and hung there. Through the surface we saw the yellow bars writhing in the wave prisms. Down below Cousteau and Laban saw the sight that was never seen before. The water was clear for a hundred feet. The dead whale rolled above in a silver halo among pink and yellow clouds of blood. Around the cage sharks patrolled like slow jet planes.

Many times Cousteau and his men had dived among sharks, but never when the scent of blood was up. They wanted to see how sharks attack. Divers must know more about sharks, their worst enemies. Cousteau could not make movies with the bars of the cage in the way. He opened the door, which is three feet wide and four feet high. Laban pulled the door upward on its hinge and tied it up. He had knife in hand, ready to cut the rope. Cousteau leaned the camera out of the door, with his head and shoulders naked to the sharks.

The wolves of the deep circled closer to the whale, getting up courage to attack. One of them broke out of the circle and swam toward the human zoo. Cousteau kept filming the white snout as it came nearer. He pulled in and the shark bumped the side of the cage. The divers in-

20. The sharks came for the divers and banged their noses on the cage bars.

stinctively looked up at their cable.

The boldest shark sniffed along the whale's side, and a battle started in the sea and in the air. The divers and sailors on deck, watching the sharks close in, grabbed spears and boathooks. The sailors lowered the diving platform to within inches of the sharks, and stood there, socking away at them in uncontrollable hatred. The first shark opened its mouth and scooped out ten pounds of whale meat in one bite. The horde attacked. They ate with their heads partly out of water. The sailors hit them with everything. The sharks ate right through it. They set their jaws into the whale and shook their powerful bodies like terriers to loosen the meat. The ocean foamed white and bloody.

Cousteau and Laban saw sharks go up beneath the whale and bite off its fins. Then a ten-foot blue shark came for the cage. The divers closed the door fast. The brute struck head on, with a heavy shock. It turned and swam away. It seemed to feel nothing. Cousteau pressed the signal buzzer and we hoisted the cage. Next Dumas and Malle went down into the nightmare.

A dozen dives in the human zoo produced the stirring scenes of the shark onslaught in the movie, *The Silent World*. The crew, still in heat of anger, began hooking sharks and hauling them out.

At last we sailed away, exhausted from the battle in the agelong war of men and sharks. Unknown to us, we carried with us other survivors of the grim day. The next time we dived, we found many remoras fastened to the ship's bottom. These sucker fish that cling to sharks had been shaken off during the whale attack and had transferred to the *Calypso*.

CHAPTER XIV

Fire Under the Sea

THE *CALYPSO* ROLLED in the Indian Ocean monsoon. Spray flew over the high radarscope. Day after day the wind and waves beat at her on the long passage from the Seychelles to Madagascar. She pounded on, with dishes breaking and white waves climbing over the sides and spraying through the tightest doors. The old saying "a sailor must keep one hand for the ship and one hand for himself" was true for the *Calypso* team. Sailing between diving locations, they usually prepare the underwater gear for the next job. But they could not work in the monsoon. Cousteau and Dumas braced against the map table in the heaving chartroom. "Our people are very tired," said Cousteau. "There is a little island near here called Assumption that might shelter us from the wind. Let's anchor for a day to get some rest and tidy up."

As soon as the *Calypso* rounded the white sand tip of Assumption, she was out of the wind. She sailed along the fringing reef and anchored in lovely calm. The boatswain

110

lowered the stern diving platform and rigged the ladder for
Dumas and Falco, who were eager to see the unknown coral
regions below.

The two tanned men finned down through still, warm
water, while the wind whipped up high, cold seas a few
miles away. Dumas and Falco nudged each other and
pointed. They could see two hundred feet through the
crystal water under Assumption Reef! Below them was a
gorgeous sloping coral bank arrayed with massive coral
domes, parasol corals, caves glowing with crimson sponges
and beds of huge anemones that looked like a giant's tomato
salad. They swam by trees of precious black coral, thickets
of pink staghorn coral and thin white sea whips standing
from the reef.

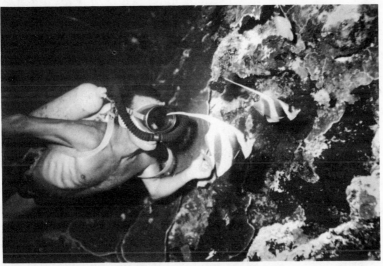

21. Dumas gets friendly with two Moorish idol fish in an Indian
Ocean reef.

Dumas and Falco had never seen so many fish in one look: black and yellow butterfly fish, lionfish with white spines eighteen inches long, blue and yellow doctor fish with sharp knives folded against their tails. Golden clown-fish darted without harm among the poisoned tentacles of the anemones. Schools of striped sergeant majors and blue snappers, wrasses and heavy sea bass, porgies and red squirrelfish, swam before their wondering eyes. The scouting party zoomed to the diving ladder. "Incredible!" Dumas reported. "Never have I seen anything like this reef!"

Cousteau said, "We'll film right here. Let's get the stuff ready. Robino and Falco, look after the Scooters. Martin, rig the underwater floodlights. Laban and Delmas, are the cameras working okay?"

Cousteau went down for a look, while the diving deck turned into a busy workshop. He came up and said, "This is a glorious spot." The team gathered around. He spoke solemnly. "We have found a wilderness where man is unknown. These fish have never seen a hook or a hunter. We have a chance for a great experiment, a peaceful invasion of the sea, to see if we can be accepted among the fish and live in their world for a while. No one is to take a spear gun. Move slowly, without rapid gestures that might scare them."

Delmas chopped some meat, put it in a cloth bag and went down. He slipped into a parade of blue-striped snappers and spread the tidbits in the water. The little fish crowded around and hundreds more hurried to the feast.

While Delmas won the friendship of the fish, those above prepared for a fire dive. Dumas brought out wooden poles about three feet long, with red rubber bags at the end, from

which wires ran to batteries on the other end. Cousteau
dived to fifty feet with a movie camera. He hung there with
the camera pointed up. Five divers carrying the poles turned
down in unison, swimming side by side, toward him.

He signaled. They pressed the triggers on the batteries.

22. Dumas with submarine torch. Battery in watertight bag at
bottom ignites chemical in top bag, burns it away, and fire flares
naked in the sea.

Suddenly the blue depths flashed with five colossal lights, each burning at over a million candlepower! Dumas-Ruggieri torches were bringing fire under the sea, the strongest underwater light except for an atomic explosion. From the torches streamed thick silver trails of bubbles, hissing and crackling in the silence. They had fired a chemical inside the waterproof rubber bag. The air in the bladder allowed the flame to catch on, then the rubber burned away and naked fire flared beneath the ocean.

Cousteau kept his camera on the fire divers and swam down after them, showing in one lengthy shot, the flight of the torch team from the surface to the sea floor 165 feet down. Five million candlepower is enough for a night football game, yet the torches lighted up the sea in a limited radius. Water swallows light very quickly.

Flash photographers also covered the peaceful invasion of Assumption Reef. Luis Marden of the National Geographic Society had a camera with two flash reflectors. His assistant carried Marden's flash bulbs in a string shopping bag. The buoyant bulbs were hung with diver's belt weights. With the bulbs flying above him, he looked like a balloon seller.

Usually the fragile bulbs withstood pressure, but once Marden went deeper than usual, and one crushed. The implosion set off the other bulbs, showering the photo team with broken glass. The weights pulled the assistant down through the sea. He let go the weights and hung in place.

Marden discovered small sand mounds that spouted occasionally like miniature volcanoes. There seemed to be buried animals making the eruptions. Marden spent several

23. Flash photographer's assistant carrying bulbs in a string bag ballasted with belt weights.

dives lying beside a mound vainly waiting to photograph an eruption. All around him the volcanoes went off, but his would not spout. Cousteau dived to see what was keeping him down so long. He saw the patient Marden lying on his belly by a mound. Cousteau pointed at it and snapped his finger. The volcano spouted. Marden was too surprised to get the picture. They moved to another volcano. Cousteau pointed, and it too erupted. Again Marden missed the shot. Then it was time to go up.

Marden followed Cousteau around the ship, saying, "Come on now, what's the trick?" Cousteau said, "It's a secret." Then he confessed, "Luis, it was just dumb luck. I was as surprised as you were."

The wonderful reef tempted them far into the blue. To

cover distances without exhaustion from swimming, they used the *Calypso's* Submarine Scooters. They are yellow electric torpedoes that pull divers along at three miles an hour, about as fast as a diver can travel underwater. Captain Saôut lowered two Submarine Scooters from the stern. One is too heavy for one man to lift, but weighs only two pounds underwater. Dumas and Falco grasped the rear handlebars. The propellers in their safety guards are lower than the divers' heads so that the slipstream doesn't tear their masks off.

They squeezed the starter levers on the right handlebars. *Wharoom!* The motors roared. The Submarine Scooters spiraled down into the twilight. They need no rudders or hydroplanes to steer by. The diver is his own rudder. By changing the angle of his body and foot fins, he makes his Scooter go wherever he pleases. He can stunt like an airplane, because he, too, flies free in a liquid element. Dumas and Falco raced across the floor. The bottom rushed past dizzily. They sped for miles, breaking through hills of golden fish, which closed formation unharmed after they were gone. They dodged around big coral heads, and drove under parasol corals.

Up they rode along the fabulous reef, its flower bed of colors blurred together by speed. They separated and drove head on at each other like two rockets about to collide in the stratosphere. At the last moment, with a twist of foot fins, they passed with a foot to spare. When you are loafing in space, looking at the many-storied reef wall, and a Submarine Scooter springs out from behind the coral and pelts toward you, that is a moment of fright and glory.

24. Two Submarine Scooters range the reef and meet messenger from the ship.

The Scooters ranged along the reef to a coral tunnel, turned and drove fifty feet through the secret life of dark ocean caverns. They burst out into the big blue and nosed down to chase a grouper across the meadow of the sea. The fish rolled its eyes, alarmed at the loud marauders. It turned and ran for a coral peak. The yellow rockets chased it into a cranny and soared up to avoid crashing.

Falco and Dumas came upon a four-foot sea turtle, rowing along in slow content. As they approached, the turtle trimmed its hind paws along its tail to streamline itself and struck out hard with its forepaws. The reptile pulled away

from them with this burst of speed, but could not keep it up
for long. Falco drove alongside, let go of his handlebars
and got on the turtle's back as neatly as a trick rider changing horses. His Submarine Scooter sank gently to the sand;
its motor cut as he released the accelerator grip.

The puzzled turtle swam hard but big Falco was a drag.
The turtle sank to the sand and floundered along. Dumas
roared past, challenging Falco to a race. But the turtle
needed a breath after its exertions. It got off the ground and
carried Falco to the surface. The turtle stuck its head out,
took a hoarse gulp of air, and dived. Falco held on, still
trying to steer the independent steed. The turtle sank to
the bottom, refusing to race. As Dumas came by, Falco let
go of the turtle and grabbed his partner's foot fins. He was

25. The hospitable Submarine Scooter team picks up some tired
divers and gives them a free ride to the Calypso.

carried in tandem to his parked Scooter. He dropped the tow, took his own handlebars and roared off after Dumas.

On the way to surface, they passed a group of pedestrian divers working on the reef, and offered them a ride. Each Submarine Scooter hauled four divers, clinging to each other's fins, up to the sun and air.

CHAPTER XV

The Great Ulysses

MAGIC DAYS PASSED as they explored and filmed Assumption Reef, virgin wilderness of the tropic sea. Captain Cousteau's peaceful invasion plan worked perfectly. The fish paid no attention to the divers. For the deep color movies they used six-thousand-watt floodlights, sometimes six of them in a single scene. If you turned one on in the air, the bulb exploded from the heat. But downstairs the water kept them cool enough.

The divers found underwater wonders such as the sea squirt, a big wormlike creature that strains food from the mud and sand it sucks in. Diver Émile Robert brought up a squirt. Two little living fish called fierasfers fell from its insides. They were not a squirt dinner; they live inside it and share the squirt's meals, privileged to go and come as they please. The team photographed blue parrot fish chewing and swallowing bites of hard coral, from which they get hidden food. The parrot fish is a living sand quarry. In goes rock, out comes sand. "Seeing how fish live is better than seeing them die on a spear," said the divers.

Groupers lived on the reef, each in his own territory from which he chased others. Dumas noticed that a large grouper more than three feet long was following him around. He faced the ugly muzzle of the fish and they looked at each other. Back on deck, Dumas said, "This guy is very interested in us. The others look us over and go on with their business, but the big one wants to watch everything."

Cousteau said, "Let's try to make a friend of him."

Groupers do not have cutting teeth like sharks. They have row after row of grinders extending from their lips back into their throats. They swallow and grind their prey.

Delmas got his picnic basket ready to go down and make friends with the grouper. He realized it would be an unhappy moment if the big fish accidentally got his grinders around his hand, but was willing to trust the animal's discretion. He found the big fish waiting for him. He held a chunk of meat in his hand and the grouper came for it. Delmas let go of the meat and the fish swept it in, inches from his hand. He held up another piece in his fingertips. The grouper gobbled it without touching his fingers. Soon the big fish swam close to them, whether they had food or not. Dumas found it loafing in the bottom grasses and swam to within two feet of the wide mouth and goggle eyes. The fish did not move. Dumas reached out his hand and scratched its head like a dog.

They named the fish Ulysses after the wandering hero of Homer's *Odyssey*. Ulysses went to them every day, begging and playing. They stroked his flanks and scratched his head. Some fish become pets in captivity and will eat from the hand, but this was an animal of the open sea that chose to become a mascot.

Although they did not exceed the time limit, the divers played extra safe against the bends by a method called stage decompression. It consists of stopping on the way up from the last dive of the day and hanging for five minutes at a depth of twenty feet to be sure you get rid of extra nitrogen. One day seven men were clinging to the *Calypso's* anchor chain. Up from the depths came Ulysses to keep them company.

The next morning, Laban, the first diver on the ladder, saw a big shape lurking two feet under the ladder. Laban ducked his mask under. "It's Ulysses," he said. "He's waiting to take us to work." Ulysses was there each morning and in the evening he swam up and stayed with them during stage decompression.

One day Delmas was swimming along the floor, feeding the little fish, when Ulysses sneaked up behind him and swallowed the whole food bag. He ran away and they did not see him again that day. The next morning they found Ulysses lying motionless on the floor, apparently in pain. His big belly was indented. It looked as though the cloth bag was twisted in his intestines. They stayed with him stroking his head, but Ulysses did not move.

The next day he was still in the same place. What could you do about a fish with indigestion? The ship's doctor said, "Don't ask me. I don't know how to treat a belly-ache a hundred feet under water." Ulysses refused food. The divers kept an eye out for sharks, lest some raider attack their helpless friend.

Ulysses was in bed four days. The sickroom was empty when they came down on the fifth day. That afternoon, they saw him at a distance. He would not come nearer. Ulysses seemed to think they had pulled a dirty trick on him. The divers were happy to see him fit and well again.

Ulysses soon forgot his grudge and came back to help out on the movie. They were photographing some little fish, when Ulysses blundered into the circle of men holding floodlights and cameras. He swam in front of the cameras, scaring the little actors and tangling with the floodlight cables. They moved to another location. Ulysses went along and hogged the camera. Their friend was becoming a nuisance.

Six weeks had passed in Assumption Reef and the divers were tired. The meat locker of the *Calypso* was exhausted and they were eating sea turtle and canned goods. Their flour was gone and fresh water was so low they did not have enough to take a shower after a dive. They were suffering from salt sores. Captain Saôut checked the remaining supplies and told Cousteau they could spend only three more days at Assumption. The gallant divers increased their efforts on the bottom. So did Ulysses. He ruined a couple more scenes.

Delmas shook his fist at his old pal. Nobody wanted to hurt Ulysses or chase him away, but something had to be done, if they were to finish the scenes. Delmas got the idea that saved the day. He went up to the *Calypso* and called to Saôut, "Send down the anti-shark cage, Skipper." Saôut instantly climbed to the boat deck. "Sharks!" he yelled to the boatswain. "Give us a hand on the cage, quick."

26. Ulysses, the grouper who became the divers' pet, grew too friendly and had to be put in jail. The anti-shark cage was his cell as the Calypso team finished the movie.

"No," Delmas said, "there are no sharks. Don't worry, Skip. No need to lower it, just throw the cage over the side." The cage dropped down to the floor. Falco held the door open. Ulysses watched this new toy with fascination. Dumas pointed at Ulysses and swept his hand toward the door. The big fish swam right in.

Clank! Ulysses was in jail. He pressed his muzzle against the bars, but did not struggle. The divers petted him through the bars, and went away to finish the picture. They were able to work without having an eighty-pound chum blunder through the studio, knocking over lights and scaring the actors.

They fed Ulysses through the bars of his cell. Above them,

the cook hooked a barracuda over the side. He is the only old-fashioned angler on the *Calypso*. The divers often swim up to his hook and give a yank and he reels in excitedly to find nothing. Or his hook comes up with an old shoe or a comic book. But this time he got a five-foot barracuda. Delmas took half of it down to Ulysses. The jailbird swallowed it in one gulp. They knew Ulysses pretty well by this time. He would never purposely harm them. But, still, the sight of thirty inches of barracuda vanishing into Ulysses in one snap made them think of their bare arms.

The movie was finished. They opened Ulysses' jail door and stood back for his dash for freedom. But Ulysses did not move. They waved for him to come out. Ulysses just looked at them. Falco went into the cage and shoved Ulysses toward the door with his foot. Reluctantly, the undersea prisoner went out into the cruel world. They had to nudge him along. His feelings seemed hurt. He swam away into the sapphire depths, looking back at the fine hotel where men had served him barracudas.

The weary team stowed their gear on board. "Won't that shower feel good in Madagascar!" Dumas said. "Me for a five-pound zebu steak," said Laban. "I keep thinking," Falco said, "we'll never in our lives see anything like this reef again." The rest agreed by their silence.

The anchor chain rattled. The motors turned. They leaned on the rail, looking over the fringing reef for the last time, at the white sands of the island, thinking of the beautiful wilderness beneath the waves, where men had lived a while with fish.

Robert said, "One of the island people is coming in a

pirogue." Cousteau said to Saôut, "Slow down, Skipper. We ought to say good-by." Laban said, "What's he got with him? He's holding up something."

"It's a big grouper."

Their hearts sank.

"It's Ulysses."

The proud islander held up the big fish for them to see. Cousteau said, "We betrayed Ulysses. We taught him to eat anything and he swallowed a dirty hook."

Falco said, "I'm not sure it's Ulysses. I'm going down to see." Cousteau said, "Stop the motors!" Falco and Laban dropped over the side. In five minutes they popped out of the water, jerking out their mouthpieces to bring the news:

"Ulysses is still there! He's okay. He came to us. We had a hard time getting rid of him." Cousteau said, "Skipper, let's get out of here fast, before that character decides to follow us home."

CHAPTER XVI

The Drop-Off Line

CAPTAIN COUSTEAU'S TWO sons began diving in the early days of Aqua-Lunging. The older boy, Jean-Michel, was seven, and his brother, Philippe, five, when their father got them small Aqua-Lungs. He, or another experienced diver, always went down with them. The boys caught baby octopuses and played with them. They speared sea urchins with picnic forks. Urchins are brown, spiny balls, living on rocks. They are practically the biggest underwater danger in the Mediterranean. If you brush against them the needles puncture your skin and break off. The spines cause swelling and festering. The Cousteau boys learned how to handle urchins and cut them open for the delicious pink eggs inside.

Jean-Michel and Philippe have gone on many *Calypso* expeditions during school vacations. Once, when they were small boys, they flew alone to Arabia to join the ship. As they landed in Jidda the *Calypso* was working with a party of scientists far out in the Abu-Latt reefs. Captain Cousteau

27. High spirits at dinner on the Calypso. At Madame Simone Cousteau's right is son Jean-Michel; at her left, son Philippe, Captain Cousteau and cook. At lower right is cameraman Louis Malle; above him American technician Robert Edgerton.

said to his wife, "We'll never get this job finished if we stop to go in for the boys. We have two more days' work. What do you think?" She said, "Let's stay on the job." She concealed her fears; her sons were alone in a town where slaves still shuffled along the streets and where a member of the ruling family can throw you in jail if he doesn't like your looks.

At last the *Calypso* reached Jidda and Mme Cousteau rushed ashore to find her boys. A limousine, flying the French flag, pulled up on the dock, and out stepped Jean-Michel and Philippe with the French Minister. Jean-Michel said, "Why are you worried, Mother? When we didn't see you at the airport, we knew you must be working hard. So we phoned the Minister and he let us stay at his house. We have been riding around, seeing all the sights."

At eighteen, Jean-Michel spent a summer working as a diver and underwater photographer at the Woods Hole Oceanographic Institution on Cape Cod, Massachusetts. He learned to square dance and flew back to Paris dressed as a cowboy. He is called "the Texas man" at his school.

Philippe designs space ships and undersea vehicles. He wants to visit the moon and the deepest place on earth, the Challenger Deep in the Pacific—nearly seven miles down. While his brother was at Woods Hole, Philippe flew to French West Africa to join the *Calypso,* which was working in the equatorial Atlantic.

The *Calypso* called at Madeira Island, where sperm whales are hunted by Portuguese boats. There Philippe joined up for a whale hunt. One day the *Calypso* met the whaler at sea. His mother saw Philippe standing on the sea behind the whaler. He yelled to her, "I'm riding a whale." She shouted back, "Be careful!" Philippe answered, "It's okay, the whale's dead." The ship was towing her catch to port and Philippe had just invented a new way to water-ski.

Captain Cousteau does not insist that his sons become underwater explorers. He says, "It's their business to find out what they want to do in life. I'll help them to get the education to do it. Then, they'll be on their own."

The family now lives in Monaco in a pink and blue villa perched on the edge of a two-hundred-foot drop to the sea. There isn't much quiet around the house. Philippe and Jean-Michel roar up on motor scooters with a gang of friends and dive into a mob of explorers and scientists inside. The first little man from Mars could drop in without being noticed. As the talk goes on, a dachshund and a white cat from Madeira chase each other through the house, boxing and wrestling.

Unnoticed in the hubbub are the trophies won by Cousteau's color film, *The Silent World*. One is an object resembling a cactus, the Grand Prize of the Cannes International Film Festival. The other is an Oscar, the Hollywood award for best feature documentary. Cousteau told a recent guest, "The movie was our farewell to the upper layers of the sea. We wanted to leave a souvenir of the beauty and adventure our team experienced in twenty years of free diving. That period is over for us. Thousands are now exploring with Aqua-Lung and scientists are using it as a regular tool of oceanographic research. The region down to two hundred feet is getting pretty busy. We must move on deeper. We are going to the continental shelf next, and after that, who knows?" He grinned. "We have some ideas for going very deep."

The parade of visitors to the pink villa are mainly concerned with the continental shelf invasion, mankind's next frontier in the sea. The shelf is three times deeper than the compressed air diving range. The shores of continents often slant out shallowly underwater for a considerable distance. This is the continental shelf. It ends at a brink called the drop-off line, around six hundred feet down. From the drop-off line the continental slope falls to the oceanic planes and abysses.

Most of the food fish live on the shelf, which is within the zone of photosynthesis, or sun chemistry. Daylight pene-

trates the shelf waters, bringing to its vegetation the same
growing processes as the sun does on land: the production
of carbohydrates essential to plants and the animals that eat
plants, and the animals that eat animals. As more and more
children are born into the world, the fish must be harvested
more efficiently to feed them.

The shelf also stores mineral and chemical riches, some
of which are already being gathered by offshore oil wells
such as the *Calypso* scouted on the Pirate Coast. What in-
terests Cousteau's undersea pioneers is how the advance
scouts are going to reach the shelf and explore it. They are
convinced that men must roam the shelf, surveying and
prospecting, although it is three times beyond the Aqua-
Lung range.

Cousteau shares his time between this adventure and a
big new job he has recently accepted as director of the
Oceanographic Museum at Monaco, the world's largest
museum and laboratory devoted to the sea. It is a short walk
through a beautiful cliffside park from his house to the great
white museum towering 280 feet above the Mediterranean.
It was founded by Prince Albert I of Monaco in 1910. He
was "the Oceanographic Prince," a real seagoing scientist
who hunted whales to study them. Once he and his Dundee
harpooner, Mr. Wedderburn, took a sperm whale whose
stomach contained a half-digested squid tentacle twenty-
seven feet long. It meant that the whole squid must have
been at least sixty-five feet long.

Cousteau assumed charge of two more research vessels
when he was elected at Monaco: the new *Winaretta Singer*
and the *Pisa III*. Through the museum, he is drawing on

the oceanographic brains of the world to join the assault on the depths. His own organizations are doing most of the work. The three naked men who plunged into the secret sea twenty years ago have now grown to a hundred. Outside of the navies, it is the world's foremost scientific diving group.

CHAPTER XVII

Diving Saucers

IN THE COMMERCIAL docks at Marseille there is a long, gray building with two cryptic signs on front: CALYPSO and OFRS. This is the underwater laboratory of the future, *l'Office Français de Recherches Sous-Marines* (OFRS), the French Undersea Research Center which Cousteau started in 1952.

Its chief is twenty-seven-year-old André Laban, chemist, engineer and diver, a tall friendly fellow who is one of Cousteau's top associates, along with Commander Jean Alinat, a veteran member of the Navy Undersea Research Group now on leave as Cousteau's executive officer. Also, Émile Gagnan, co-inventor of the Aqua-Lung, has continued working with Cousteau and the OFRS on underwater devices.

Laban recently took me around the little-known OFRS lab. In the carpentry and plastics shop, engineers were building sleek, small underwater cameras and electric Submarine Scooters. They had already built the world's best

133

underwater television camera with engineers of the Thomson-Houston Company. TV can photograph further underwater than a diver can see. Not satisfied with that, the OFRS added a new optional system that makes TV able to penetrate turbid waters.

Our tour was interrupted by shouting on the docks: "The *Calypso* is in!" The research ship sidled in, threw her monkey fist, and men hauled the big bights of the mooring cables over the quayside bollards. The *Calypso* crew yelled greetings to Captain Joe Toscano, skipper of the OFRS research boat, the *Espadon* (swordfish). People poured out of the vessels and held a noisy reunion with their pals in the workshop. Technicians, scientists, sailors and divers are all the same in Cousteau's organization. They take turns going to sea and working ashore. Greeting Albert Falco was Professor Jacques Chouteau, a distinguished young nuclear scientist of the University of Aix-Marseille, who studies "rapture of the deep" and is a diver himself. Here was the central design group of the OFRS: engineers Sivirine and Mollard and draftsmen Strada and Folco. Others on hand were Élie Ferrat, the treasurer of the OFRS and also president of the French Federation of Diving Clubs; big Yves Girault, a real estate man, who runs the OFRS sports section, training young divers and spreading underwater sportsmanship codes; and Armand Davso, technician and diver, a city employee loaned to the OFRS.

They are not penned up in the labs; the OFRS conducts daring expeditions of its own.

The OFRS has explored the underground river at Port-Miou, which empties into the Mediterranean sixty feet

down. The diving teams strung electric lights 350 feet into
the river and leapfrogged deeper with surveying equipment
and portable lights. They penetrated 625 feet inside. It was
the longest swim beneath the earth. They could not go
further. They had to save enough air to get back.

Girault, the real estate man, led the deepest cave dives
on record, by an OFRS expedition in the Fountain of
Vaucluse in 1955. In this water cave in 1947 Cousteau and
Dumas came nearest to losing their lives on a dive. Unknown
to them, their air compressor had been sucking in its own
exhaust fumes and filling the Aqua-Lung bottles with a
deadly percentage of carbon monoxide. Dumas passed out
nearly two hundred feet down. Cousteau, holding on to life
with supreme will power, dragged himself and Dumas to
the surface.

The OFRS divers returned to Vaucluse with four truck-
loads of special equipment. They strung underwater lights
down to 150 feet and lowered a loud-speaker and hydro-
phone to talk with the surface. They carried two-hundred-
watt searchlights with lighthouse lenses into the darkness
below, progressively mapping the cave as they advanced.
One hundred and eighty feet down, Kientzy and Goiran discovered a side tunnel and swam 150 feet into it without
finding an end. After eighty dives, the team reached a huge
water-filled chamber 212 feet down. The named it *La
Grande Salle des Ténèbres*. The last word means night,
mystery and gloom. Louis Malle made movies in this Great
Hall of Night at a depth of 278 feet, the deepest pictures
ever taken by a diver.

These men of the OFRS are setting out to explore the

continental shelf. Existing methods of diving are not suitable to take them there. Free divers cannot reach such depths. Observation chambers lowered from ships would be too clumsy. The bathyscaphe is too big: she was built for great depth and would be wasted on this relatively shallow exploration. To Cousteau the ideal shelf submarine would have to be a free diver with a pressure-resistant shell around him, a small and handy vehicle that could be carried around the world on the *Calypso*. The shell would move freely in all directions, or hover, so that the diver could see all around and pick up objects.

Cousteau and the OFRS designed this shelf vehicle, which was backed by the National Geographic Society, the Edo Foundation and Air Liquide. It is known as "the diving saucer." Three diving saucers are being built by the OFRS.

They look like comic book "flying saucers." The difference is that Cousteau's vehicles of inner space actually exist. He and Laban showed one to me in Marseille. Cousteau said, "There is practically nothing classic in the design." Laban translated, "We did not use previous principles of submarines." Cousteau said, "There are no propellers. The diving saucer is ellipsoidal, a flattened sphere. Unlike submarines, the diving saucer has underwater viewing ports, and there are hydraulic claws on the outside, operated by remote control."

The shelf submarine is scheduled for its first underwater tests about the time this book appears. Even as the diving saucer begins the invasion of the continental shelf, Cousteau's group is working on ways to go far deeper.

CHAPTER XVIII

To the Abyss

CAPTAIN COSTEAU IS surprised at people who consider space satellites and rockets as the frontier of exploration. "I wonder why we are dreaming of space when we know nothing about what is under our feet inside the earth," he says. "We seem to forget that seven tenths of our own planet remains unknown."

The oceans cover 71 per cent of the earth's surface and contain a thousand times more living space than the land. If you dumped all the land into the seas, the earth would be covered by water two miles deep. If you were able to look at the world from space, you would see so much water that you would call it "the ocean," rather than "the earth."

Nobody can calculate how many animals are in the sea. One branch of coral is made up of a million animals called polyps. There are quite probably more porpoises in the oceans than there are human beings on land, and there are nearly three billion of us. The sea contains the smallest animals that have ever lived and the largest animal that has ever lived—the mighty blue whale a hundred feet long. There are at least twenty-one thousand species of marine fish, and around a hundred new ones are being discovered each year, many by free divers. Scientists working from the *Calypso* have found several dozen new species and have given three of them scientific names ending in *cousteauii,* in honor of the explorer.

The vast ocean mantle is virtually a living thing itself. Its global system of currents and winds decides climate and weather. Take the warm Gulf Stream, flowing north along the U.S. Atlantic Coast; it eventually reaches a tentacle to the Scilly Islands in Britain, causing palm trees to grow in the same latitude as Bureya, Siberia.

Geophysicists form theories on the creation and structure of the earth, knowing very little about the seven tenths underwater. Oceanographers are today sending instruments to great depths to get bottom samples, temperature readings and the speed of deep currents, but, compared with the infinity of the oceans, these are touches in the dark. Cousteau believes men must go to abysses to see for themselves. He is a "see-it-yourself" oceanographer.

The average depth of the oceans is about two and a half miles. This was once reached by the French bathyscaphe in a brief dive, but the depths remain as a challenge to the spirit of science and exploration.

The greatest depth yet discovered is well-named the Challenger Deep. It is in the Mariana Trench, two hundred miles southwest of Guam Island in the western Pacific. The bottom was echo-sounded by the British Navy survey ship, H.M.S. *Challenger,* as 35,640 feet deep. It would take a cannon ball sixty-two minutes to sink in the Challenger Deep. If you dropped Mount Everest into the water here, you would have to dive a mile to reach the summit where Tensing and Hilary stood.

Cousteau believes men will go to the "Everest of the Sea," not as a stunt, but as trained observers with cameras and instruments to bring back vital information on the subcellar of the globe. For instance, they will have gravity meters to measure the thickness of the earth's crust at the world's lowest point. The depth argonauts may be able to test the theory that the crust is thinnest at the deepest place. No one will ever be able to get closer to the core of the earth than the divers of the Challenger Deep.

The abyssal explorers will have to go down inside a sphere, the strongest of pressure-resistant shapes. They will be combating pressure more than a thousand times stronger than that of the normal atmosphere. It will exert a force of more than fifteen thousand pounds on every square inch of the ball.

Yet we know that there are naked little animals alive in such pressures! The Danish Galatea Expedition dredged anemones and sea cucumbers from a depth of thirty-three thousand feet in the Philippine Trench. Perhaps there are larger swimming animals in the abyss. Houot and Willm saw sharks 13,287 feet down in the eastern Atlantic on the big dive of the *FNRS 3*.

Captain Cousteau and Dr. Edgerton are already scouting ahead of the abyssal divers with flash cameras that withstand enormous pressures. During the Calypso Equatorial Atlantic Expedition in 1956, they made automatic electronic flash photos twenty-five thousand feet down in the Romanche Trench. They were the deepest photos ever taken. Edgerton's newest camera was built to withstand the pressure of the Challenger Deep.

The Challenger dive is taking years of preparation by the scientific adventurers. It will take several specially equipped mother ships and a constant meteorological scouting in the air. The greatest hazards of the big dive will be on the surface. The waters above the Challenger Deep are too rough for diving most of the year. The only days of flat calm are during the hurricane season. So the secrets of the deepest place on earth will have to be sought between hurricanes!

The first man to look out in the abyss will have taken a long journey since the day Cousteau first ducked his diving mask underwater and stood up transformed, exultant and dedicated to exploring this greater world through all his days.

GOOD UNDERSEA READING

True Adventures

CLARK, EUGENIE *Lady With a Spear,* New York, 1952. A small, beautiful girl diver, who is also a devoted biologist, tells of undersea hunting for science.

COUSTEAU, J.-Y. and DUMAS, F. *The Silent World,* New York, 1953. The classic story of their first fifteen years under the sea by the founders of Aqua-Lung diving.

CRAIG, JOHN D. *Danger Is My Business,* New York, 1938. Starting as a helmet diver and underwater movie photographer, Colonel Craig's adventurous life is an honest picture of diving.

GILPATRIC, GUY *The Compleat Goggler,* New York, 1957. Brave and funny story by a great free-diving pioneer of thirty years ago, who inspired many early divers.

GROSSETT, HARRY *Down to the Ships in the Sea,* London, 1953. A veteran helmet diver writes his reminiscences at seventy. A grand, truthful book about a life of underwater labor.

HOUOT, GEORGES, and WILLM, PIERRE *2000 Fathoms Down,* New York, 1955. The master of the deep-boat and his shipmate recount the world's record dives of the French Navy bathyscaphe.

TAILLIEZ, PHILIPPE *To Hidden Depths*, New York, 1954. The fascinating third man of the Cousteau-Dumas team tells his fine story of their adventures.

General History

DAVIS, ROBERT H. *Deep Diving and Submarine Operations*, London, 1951 (fifth edition). The old man of the sea, for seventy-five years a submarine engineer, makes a monumental book of history and reference.

DUGAN, JAMES *Man Under the Sea*, New York, 1956. The author of *Undersea Explorer* writes a history of underwater discovery, photography, archeology, submarines, etc.

Diving Guides with Diving Tables

OWEN, DAVID M. *A Manual for Free Divers*, London and New York, 1955. A short, reliable guide by the chief diver and underwater photographer of the Woods Hole Oceanographic Institution.

UNDERSEA RESEARCH GROUP, FRENCH NAVY *The Complete Guide to Free Diving*, New York, 1957. The best Aqua-Lung manual by the men who pioneered it, including Cousteau, Tailliez, Dumas, etc.

Diving Magazines

SKIN DIVER, THE (monthly), PO Box 128, Lynwood, California. The original American diving paper and organ of the diving clubs. It carries international underwater news.